A QUICK TING ON...
...ABOUT THE SERIES

A Quick Ting On is an idea rooted in archiving all things Black British culture. It is a book series dedicated to Black Britishness and all the ways this identity expands and grows. Each book in the series focuses on a singular topic that is of cultural importance to Black Britishness (and beyond), giving it the sole focus it deserves. The series was inspired by everyday conversations had with Black British folk far and wide, whether that be in WhatsApp group chats, in person, on social media, at parties, barbecues and so on.

A Quick Ting On is about providing an arena for Black people to archive things that they deem important to them and in turn allowing these explorations to exist long after we are here.

A bundle of joy, learning, nostalgia and home.

Magdalene Abraha FRSA (Mags)
xx

PRAISE FOR
A QUICK TING ON...

'Groundbreaking,' *The Guardian*

'Amazing,' *The Metro*

'Timely and needed,' BBC Radio 5

'Spearheaded by the hugely impressive Magdalene Abraha, the heartening launch of a phenomenal new series,' Mellville House

'There is nothing like this,' *The Bookseller*

'What better way to begin Black History Month than with the announcement of a book series celebrating Black British life?' *Bustle* Magazine

'Magdalene Abraha will launch her long-awaited book series, *A Quick Ting On...* it's brilliant,' *Elle*

'Exciting,' *Refinery29*

'The first ever non-fiction book of its kind', *The Voice*

'*A Quick Ting On...* is set to be behind some of the most exciting books.' *Stylist* Magazine

'A game changer,' BBC World Service

'Bringing Black Britishness to the fore,' *The Blacklist*

'How much do you know about plantains? Or Black British Businesses? Or Afrobeats? If your answer is not enough, that could soon be rectified,' *Evening Standard*

A QUICK TING ON...

AFROBEATS

CHRISTIAN
ADOFO

AQ
TO

JACARANDA

This edition first published in Great Britain 2022
Jacaranda Books Art Music Ltd
27 Old Gloucester Street,
London WC1N 3AX
www.jacarandabooksartmusic.co.uk

A CIP catalogue record for this book is available from the British
Library

ISBN: 9781913090517
eISBN: 9781913090548

Cover Illustration: Camilla Ru
Cover Design: Baker, bplanb.co.uk
Typeset by: Kamillah Brandes

FOR FAYE

CONTENTS

PREFACE

Ever since I began my author journey, a lot has happened within and around this thing we call Afrobeats. As a fan and keen observer this has been both exciting and inspiring. It is after all a writer's dream (or nightmare) to have the subject you are writing about develop so rapidly. To my knowledge this is the first book on Afrobeats as a whole. I have been writing on the subject for over 10 years now and seeing the world catch on is something that fills me with joy.

This book will examine and celebrate the diversity of this cultural phenomenon - its key moments, its central figures, its internationality, and its likely legacy. Much will continue to develop within Afrobeats, it may even be the case that by the time this book is published, many things in the scene will be different, but my hope is this book will assert the vitality and importance of a musical culture that has made a glorious dent in the world.

The term Afrobeats over the years has become an interestingly loaded term, with connotations and meanings as diverse as its sounds and history. For me, as the son of Ghanaian migrants, born and raised in the UK, Afrobeats in many ways is part of who I am.

Afrobeats represents many things (which we will get into). It is deeper than a musical genre, it is a profound cultural fusion, one that encompasses the intersection of being born in the West whilst being raised in a West African home. Its foundation is rooted in reimagining what it means to be young, gifted and Black in the 21st century.

For the children of African migrants who are fluent in their mother tongue or at the very least understand the key phrases, Afrobeats presents a powerful space. It is a visceral and enticing opportunity to engage with our culture in an accessible and unapologetic manner far removed from any academic 'higgy-hagga'.

For diasporic West Africans, Afrobeats is the sound that connects the past to the present. A marriage of the new to the old. It personifies long standing traditions told in iconic West African songs but in new and invigorating ways. When inspecting traditional West African tracks, we often find they are tributes to truth, at times providing social commentary on socio-political issues or giving listeners valuable life lessons.

Before we continue I must assert that there is a difference between Afrobeat and Afrobeats, which will be expanded on as the book continues.

Simply put for now, Afrobeat (without the S), led by the legend that is Fela Kuti, is the musical parent who left Africa and found solace abroad in the confident African-American cousins of funk and soul. Afrobeat defined what it meant to be unapologetically African within the continent and abroad. Afrobeats (with the S) is its youngest offspring, which acknowledges the past via classic samples and familiar drum patterns in hybrid electronic form whilst maintaining the sentiment of African pride.

The genre and its many branches are centred around the world's second biggest continent. For those that share a direct connection to Africa or are floating in oceans of ambiguity as an 'other', retracing their steps back home, Afrobeats makes you proud to say you are indeed an African.

Typically, we have had to fight to have our story told correctly and respectfully. Whether it be the lazy mispronunciations of African names on the school register. Or the ease of which Band Aid and Comic Relief shaped popular discourse on the relationship between Africa and the West. Or the ignorant questions African children faced in school, 'does your family live in a hut?' or, 'is it true you live with animals?'

These perceptions of Africa and Africans coloured our experiences growing up, seeping into the subconscious of our young minds. We would hold our breaths in angst hoping it would not be our parents' country mentioned in an urgent broadcast appeal this time round. As children of West Africans, we were made to feel ashamed of our parents' strong accents and culture. At times, this embarrassment would lead to youngsters denying their African heritage and instead claiming to be from the Caribbean. This was the cultural burden placed on many first-generation British-born youngsters of African heritage. Despite our parents' upbringing and their assertions that our motherland was to be heralded with pride, everywhere else told us otherwise. It would be some years before it was cool to be African.

Originating from West Africa, with London at the epicentre, Afrobeats reflects the nuances of the Black experience a few generations after our parents struggled to settle abroad. With its foundation rooted far from the bustling city that is London, Afrobeats is a vibrant musical culture bouncing to and from cities like Lagos and Accra, amongst many others.

I hope the words in this book will resonate with those who have memories soundtracked by music their African parents played. This is for the kids who couldn't 'learn the language' but were swayed by the hypnotic melodies and magic drums of African music. This is for the people who grew up silently watching family and friends dance in hall parties before they felt confident enough to do the same. This is also for those curious to follow the lineage of Afrobeats from the motherland, recognising its popularity is much more than the 'hottest new thing'. Afrobeats has depth, sunshine and an unwavering glow, providing the reality and dynamism of what it means to be an African irrespective of one's birth place.

The origin of this book has two layers. One that involves a talented friend and music producer, Brendan Opoku Ware aka Hagan, who recommended me to Mags aka Magdalene Abraha, a writer, publisher and friend who was on the search for a writer who could tell the journey of this evolving phenomenon and its influence.

Then there is the other layer that started over 10 years ago when I began actively connecting with my African heritage post-university. So in that sense this is the book I have been working toward my whole life.

I remain grateful to Afrobeats for many reasons, for one, this music was able to eloquently capture my experience of occupying a dual identity despite being based in one location. Afrobeats for many of us became another facet of home. When my peers and I would attend university raves it was the explosive Afrobeats set that would set the crowd ablaze, yet the charts and the music industry did not reflect this. Instead we found solace in social media platforms where viral videos of people azontoing or shaku-ing to the latest Afrobeats song would be shared far and wide.

For further context, this period of the early Noughties was a strange time for me and my friends, as far as music was concerned. I distinctly remember a number of grime and UK rap artists deciding to alter their sound to cross over to the pop market. It was a dramatic change to say the least and one that at the time I found perplexing. This musical identity crisis coupled with the World Cup being in South Africa—the first time the tournament was hosted on the continent—were huge catalysts for me and, I imagine, other children of African migrants to reconnect with the culture further.

From a British perspective, Afrobeats has given the children of West Africa a new roar. Now, almost everywhere we look we see artists who look like us, have African names like us and who dance like us climbing the charts. Afrobeats provides us with something contemporary and cultural to be proud of. Something that means when the next generation of west Africans are asked, 'where are you from?' they will reply proudly.

This book seeks to acknowledge and link the landmark moments that have influenced West African singing style and rhythms, exploring how they have effortlessly crossed over to become a global juggernaut. *A Quick Ting On: Afrobeats* pays homage to the growing musical discography of a mighty sub-genre, from its mesmerising dances, to its equally enthralling adlibs and melodies. Most of all, I hope to inspire ownership of our narrative as Black people, specifically when it comes to the representation of African art and culture.

Afrobeats was loved by us before she became mainstream, before your favourite rapper jumped on one of her songs, before labels and music institutions saw her financial lucrativeness. We heard and saw ourselves in Afrobeats, we heard and saw our parents in Afrobeats, our siblings and our friends. It has grown with us and taken us to places we never imagined.

From West Africa to the world—here we are.

1

MY PERSONAL RELATIONSHIP WITH AFROBEATS

Long before our communities required us to refer to our elder family friends as aunties and uncles. Long before we assumed our default roles as the official in-house translators for our parents. Long before the heated debates over which rice grain tastes better in jollof (hint: It rhymes with Illuminati). Nigerian Afrobeat and Ghanaian highlife were the roaring soundtracks that aided many West African migrants when settling into new and often cold lands.

For children of West African migrants, weekends were two-day retreats to reconnect with 'aunty', 'uncle' and your favourite of their children. These days would be filled with warm memories of family friends who pronounced your full name with the vim of your mother. The music played at these family functions would be laced with classic proverbs and subtle metaphors, staying true to the oral storytelling tradition of Africa. In these safe spaces of home, hope was marinated so deep into consciousness that racial microaggressions and stereotypes about Africa wouldn't affect the newer bodies our parents were to birth and nurture *abroachie* (abroad in Akan language).

Our parents christened us with names that provided us with a grounding, a root to a place where the majority look just like us.

Hyphenated identities like Black-British, Black-African, or Black-other for us, would become the required way to describe our heritage on awkward census forms. Questions surrounding our identity would grow louder as we grew up in countries that didn't celebrate us like we were celebrated when we were at home, church and hall parties.

Who are we?
Who are we?
Who are we?

FROM BROADWATER FARM TO LAMBETH TOWN HALL: THE HALL PARTY EXPERIENCE

This was the sound of sunshine; it vibrated from each corner of the hall. This hall, however, was no ordinary hall. No, this hall was carved out especially for us, with rich smells of a cuisine that we couldn't wait to consume and women who looked so joyous, you couldn't help but smile. Awkwardly, we would stare into the VHS camera, where the 'videoman' would zoom in à la Google Earth (owing to alcohol intolerance). This was the hall party of all hall parties and there I was in my oversized Sunday best, assured by my extended family that I would 'grow into it.' I was Mumsy's No. 1 non-mover, stiffly perched against the wall perusing how the bodies of my family and friends magically moved to the hypnotic drum patterns of our music. Eventually the ancestors would warmly push me into the periphery of the dancing circle. They would pull my limbs and shoulders in an attempt to capture the rhythm needed for the skanking* showdown I was to partake in.

Sundays after Catholic Church were for respite. A much needed pause before the imminent mist of Monday and the new school week. Uncle** Francis aka Money Matters entered the narrow corridor of our flat. His high top was freshly cut, his eyes redly stern and his fetish for black leather clearly visible as his long trench coat laced the floor of the corridor. The Sankofa Santa brought brown paper bags filled with imported CD's (remember 'em?). With sheer enthusiasm, he would exclaim, "LATEST" whilst pulling a new CD from the bag.

His eclectic collection had it all, it was African music in a bag! Almost every album cover was illustrated with Windows '97 Word Art fonts featuring colours that made no sense whatsoever. This was our family's weekly music session. We would all bond over lyrics that my siblings and I didn't always understand, but that never mattered because the familiar foundation of polyrhythms, organ chords and digital brass were home to us. This would become an early intensive course in music criticism for me and siblings. These CD's would be played at an array of forthcoming family celebrations including but not limited to birthdays, christenings, graduations, weddings and everything in between.

In hindsight some of the safest spaces I have ever experienced were decaying church halls, overcrowded living rooms, the Broadwater Farm Community Centre and anywhere else that had a framed picture of the Akwabba*** woman pinned to the wall. These spaces were all epicentres of a mini GH****. Even though we were immersed in an African environment

---

*	to dance to the music
**	not blood related relative but uttered as sign of respect for elders
***	'welcome' in the Twi dialect
****	a colloquial abbreviation for Ghana simply using the first two letters

at home, our after-school evenings were still spent watching American hip hop and R&B music videos; back then this was the music that appealed more to our young minds. Our palette for African polyrhythms was yet to mature, but our parents would be sure to change that.

Daddy Lumba. Nakorex. Kojo. Antwi. Pat Thomas. George Darko. C.K. Mann. A.B. Crentsil are just some of the names that transport me back to this time.

GOING 'BACK' AND COMING 'BACK'.

Routine summer trips back to Ghana in my late teens humbled me and my brothers. Cockerels and the cries of every church denomination replaced what we knew as alarm clocks. Mosquitoes would feast on our uninitiated fresh skin like we were buffets. It was an experience that meant we walked every-where, breaking pedometer world records and pit stopping every few metres to greet extended relatives who would stare inquisitively and question our heritage in Twi dialect.

Upon returning to London, hall parties no longer enticed me. Like any clueless teenager, I began seeking independence which brought with it a heavy reluctance to accompany my mum to hall parties, functions on either ends of the Victoria Line. It seemed I wasn't the only one, my friends had also developed the same disengagement. At the time, I ignorantly thought my love affair with hall parties was over. I had figured this was a natural development of growing up. So, me and my peers would go on the search for alternative activities that aligned with our teenhood and sense of independence away from our parents. In my case this meant immersing myself at music festivals sponsored by cheap lager brands.

THE TEENS TO THE UK FUNKY
UNIVERSITY EXPERIENCE

The soundtracks of my formative years were filled with the early rise of a genre called hiplife* with artists like Reggie Rockstone, Obrafour and Tic-Tac. For me, this music was familiar and reminded me of home and because of that it didn't excite me at the time. It wasn't until my teens, when my younger sibling introduced me to a new cross-continental sound via his regular mixes and MP3 blog downloads that things began to change. This sound would become known as UK Funky House. This discovery was coupled with the visual representation of the Black Stars, Ghana's national men's football team playing at their first ever World Cup in 2006. Strange as it was, this triggered something in me and I started to solidify my bond to the motherland. It was thrilling to watch a football team that looked much like the men I had grown up with. The Black Stars would celebrate goals with infectious choreography which would later be shared across all forms of social media These men moved like the family and friends I had grown up with. They were on the international stage as extensions of us

Then came my university experience, which housed another significant period in the development of my cultural identity. Early UK funky house raves brought the copious catalogue of skanks and bootleg instrumentals converted into air horn anthems. The dance floor finally brought those of African descent to the forefront, after being in the contemporary musical shadow of our West Indian brethren for quite some time. Funky house, sonically, was something we had heard remnants of in our homes. Funky house would become

---

*   Ghanaian musical style which fuses hip hop, reggae and dancehall with local dialect and drum rhythms

the sound of Afro-Caribbean societies (ACS's) throughout the country, colouring every Black university cook up, drink up and rave in sight.

UK funky house MCs spraying* in languages such as Pidgin, Twi and Yoruba was reminiscent of the old-school hall party MC. This would be the first time I saw parts of the musical Africanness I was exposed to as a child outside of the home.

Upon leaving university with a clear sense of my African identity, I picked up a pen and started writing. One of my first blog posts was on highlife and hiplife songs, which I recalled from my early experience of hall parties. I wrote about what these songs meant to me growing up. A year later, I wrote an article for *The Guardian* titled, 'Black Artists: You have to know where you're from', where I spoke to British artists of African descent, such as Skepta and Estelle, about songs that reminded them of home. This period would be coupled with the early rise of a new iteration that would be called Afrobeats. In the UK, Afrobeats would bring with it a different intersection of class, identity and race, one that was for the first time rooted solely in Africanness.

So, like most who have West African parents in the West, my relationship with this cultural phenomenon and its subsequent subgenres represents home. The question is: 'how does one describe a sound/s or movement that embodies home?'

---

*   rapping

2

FELA AND AFROBEAT—
THE MAN
AND THE MUSIC

In a recent documentary, *One Day Go Be One Day*, by Akinola Davies Jr, the eldest son of Fela Kuti, Femi—himself an accomplished musician—remarked that his famous father, was close to his [Fela Kuti's] mother due to their shared political beliefs. Fela Kuti's mother held a great deal of importance to Fela Kuti, both in childhood and in adulthood. In many ways she was his ideological anchor. When describing the impact of Fela Kuti's mother's death on Fela himself, Femi explained it, 'destabilised him a bit, but this destabilisation made him stronger.'

Funmilayo Ransome-Kuti is often revered as the mother of the visionary Fela Kuti. Yet when we delve into her life we find that she is equally deserving of recognition Ransome-Kuti's role in shaping early Pan-Africanism, connecting the Black struggle across the West is in a similar vein to Caribbean contemporaries like Una Marson and Amy Ashwood Garvey.

In 1946, Ransome-Kuti set up the Abekouta Women's Union in Nigeria, bringing middle and working class women together to challenge unfair taxation from the colonial British government. Aware of her privilege as an aristocrat in the well-heeled sections of Nigerian society, she promoted women's rights to education, employment and political representation. After a lack of progress with her cause at home, she would take a two month trip to London in 1947, where she would write about the life of Nigerian women in several British newspapers, including the Communist Party newspaper *Daily Worker*. She would articulate the exploitative relationship between her nation and the 'mother country', exposing the contradiction in Britain's own fight for gender equality at home but not in the Commonwealth.

Upon her return to Nigeria, Ransome-Kuti led large scale peaceful protests with over 20,000 members of her union, which culminated in the Alake (King) of Egbaland abdicating from the throne in 1949. A model organisation for women's rights in Nigeria, Africa and across the world, this forthright and natural approach to inequality would parallel with her third born Fela Kuti's own journey in affirming his identity and speaking his truth against colonial masters.

In 1958, Fela Kuti was sent to London by his parents to study medicine and follow the lineage of his medical doctor brothers, Beko and Olikoye. Staying true to himself, he took a creative detour and enrolled at the Trinity School of Music (known as Trinity Laban today). Just as political activism ran in the Kuti family, so did music. Fela Kuti's grandfather Josiah-Jesse (JJ) was an Anglican priest who saw music as a powerful way of attracting people to the church. Interestingly, his commitment to improving the quality of church music led to him being one of the first West Africans to translate Christian hymns into Yoruba. In 1925, JJ became the first Nigerian to release a record album of gospel songs under Zonophone Records. A piano left by JJ would be the first instrument Kuti would play in the family home.

After growing tired of learning about classical European composers, this early period in London led to Fela Kuti forming the first lineup of Koola Lobitos, a highlife-influenced jazz band. Inspired by Nigerian highlife band leaders Rex Jim

Lawson and Victor Olaiya, Kuti's Koola Lobitos band began performing in venues popular with fellow African students and workers. Another influential figure on the young Fela was jazz and trap drummer Bayo Martins, who served as his mentor, enabling him to see the similarities between jazz and highlife, a musical link that would prove to be transformational for Kuti's career.

When he returned home, he returned to the newly formed Federation of Nigeria in 1963, 3 years after the country gained independence from Britain. Kuti would get a job as a junior producer at Nigeria's National Broadcasting Corporation. However, the job wouldn't fulfil the creative urges of Kuti.

The decades between 1940–1970 were periods of huge change within Africa, with many nations housing anti-colonial movements and attaining independence. This would come with a range of charismatic and passionate African leaders including Nkrumah (Ghana), Kenyatta (Kenya) and Banda (Malawi), all of whom were educated abroad and would become the leaders of their newly independent nations. As an African also educated abroad, Kuti's return home bore similar sentiments. Fuelled by racism and colonial relations in London, Kuti was happy to be back in Nigeria. Kuti, like Nkrumah, Banda and Kenyatta was a representation of the empowered African controlling narratives long suffocated by racial subordination. It should also be noted that this period saw a number of prominent African-Americans, including W.E.B. Dubois and Maya Angelou, visiting Africa.

Kuti's views on taboo topics, including government corruption and contradictions in African society, were beginning to flow through the music he created with his band. Around this time Kuti formed a fresh lineup of his band Koola Lobitos, this would include the addition of Tony Allen on drums, Tunde Williams on trumpet and Yinka Roberts on guitar, amongst other new band members.

The aforementioned Nigerian highlife musicians Rex Jim Lawson and Victor Olaiya were influenced by the Ghanian genre of highlife. They were particularly inspired by Ghanaian musician E.T Mensah and his band the Tempos, who first toured Nigeria in 1950 with their independence-themed songs to unite the population's struggle for freedom. For Fela Kuti, who was 12 years old at the time, there is no doubt that this would have all had a huge influence on the music he was to make in future decades. In 1968, Fela took a tour to Ghana, the home of highlife, accompanied by his first manager, Benson Idonije (Burna Boy's grandfather). Kuti's music was well received by both Ghanaian audiences and musicians alike. It is believed that it was here that Fela Kuti coined the term 'Afrobeat'. Writer and archivist John Collins explains, 'the word Afrobeat was invented in Accra by Fela, it wasn't in Nigeria. He [Kuti] actually coined the name because he wanted to distinguish his name from soul [music].'

Frustrated that his music didn't crossover with audiences in his home country, Fela Kuti left for the United States for ten months to tour in 1969 with the Koola Lobitos. Kuti would temporarily settle in Los Angeles, where he would come into contact with a woman called Sandra Izsadore. Izsadore was an African-American civil rights activist who was a member of the Black Panther Party. She would inspire Kuti to reflect on the militant ethos of the Black Panther movement and embrace his African roots wholeheartedly. Speaking to the Cuban writer Carlos Moore in his authorized biography *Fela: This Bitch of a Life*, Kuti stated, 'Sandra gave me the education I wanted. She was the one who opened my eyes, talked to me about politics, history… She blew my mind really.' It would be Fela Kuti's epiphanic conversations with Izsadore that would be the catalyst for his track, 'My Lady Frustration', taken from the infamous *'69 L.A. Sessions* album. Despite being away from home at the time of the song's creation, Kuti would declare it his first 'African' tune. The song would be an early template for what would become the Afrobeat genre.

The American tour was an educational experience for a 31-year-old Fela Kuti. Izsadore would create an extensive reading list for Kuti which included works by a plethora of African-American figures, including Nikki Giovanni, Angela Davis and Malcolm X.

In 1970, Kuti decided to leave America for Nigeria after a promoter failed to obtain work permits for members of the Koola Lobitos. Kuti left America with a heightened sense of political consciousness, which he reflected on in a 1977 *New York Times* interview: 'It was incredible how my head was turned. Everything fell into place, man. For the first time, I saw the essence of Blackism (Black Nationalism)… I had no country, just a bunch of Africans running around in suits trying to be Englishmen. I decided to come back and try to make my country African.'

Kuti arrived 'back home' ready to bring about change. In 1971, in Nigeria, Kuti changed the name of his band the Koola Lobitos to Africa 70. With the new name came a fresh lineup of musicians. Fela Kuti's methodical approach as a bandleader coupled with a permanent space at the Afro-Spot venue in Lagos would build a foundation for some of the most important events in African musical history.

Another significant consequence of his time across the Atlantic was Kuti's decision to drop 'Ransome' from his surname. To Kuti, the name 'Ransome' was a colonial arte-fact that reminded him of his family's connection to slavery. He decided to replace it with 'Anikulapo', which is Yoruba for 'one who has captured death and put it in his pouch'. This occurrence parallels with a similar experience in Malcolm X's life where he too chose to reject his slave name changing his surname from 'Little' to 'X.' The rejection of 'slave names' or 'colonial names' was a growing occurence amongst Black people across the world who understood of the ills of slavery and colonialism. For Kuti, this title transformation was the final part of his personal and musical reinvention.

In an excerpt from the documentary *Faces of Africa—Fela Kuti: The Father of Afrobeat*, Kuti's shift in musical consciousness was epitomised in an archive clip where he said, 'if you are in England, the music can be an instrument of enjoyment. You can sing about love... But in my own environment, my society is undeveloped because of an alien [colonial] system on our people. There is something like a struggle for people's existence'

Kuti's early experiences of migration to the UK and US emboldened him to recognise how colonialism affected Black people across the globe. His ability to offer clear commentary on this issue via his music would start a tumultuous relationship between himself and the Nigerian government.

His newly formed group Africa 70 came with a highly impressive lineup of talented artists. Tenor saxophonist Igo Okweichere, guitarist Fred Lawal, percussionist Henry 'Perdido' Kofi and the acclaimed brilliance of drummer Tony Allen. Now in a new musical phase, Fela Kuti would use nights at a Lagos venue called The Afro-Spot to test his new songs on live audiences.

Another new feature of Kuti's performances were his 'yabi' sessions. The term 'yabi' originates from Pidgin English meaning to make fun of something or someone. Kuti's 'yabi' sessions would be long spoken sections within his songs where he would joke about himself and the audience. He would often use these sessions to address socio-political issues occuring in Nigeria. He soon renamed The Afro-Spot to The Africa

Shrine in 1974. The venue became a cultural hub that regularly attracted a large number of Nigerians.

Even at this time the West African music industry was dominated by Western record companies including EMI, Decca and Phillips/Phonogram. Understanding the power of music labels, Kuti encouraged a bidding war for his independently recorded discography. He also dictatedl the manner in which much of his music was marketed and shared .

In Lindsay Barrett's essay for *The Wire*, Barrett reflects on Kuti's unorthodox but effective marketing strategy: 'He would go into the EMI studios in Apapa (Nigeria) and produce extended versions of two of the group's [Africa 70] most popular and topical compositions. EMI would release the songs immediately, their remarkable sales [would be] fueled by the fact that a few weeks after they were issued on vinyl, Fela would stop singing them in his club.'

THE MUSIC

'Gentleman', from the self-titled album released in 1973, comments on the colonial mentality of Africans who were tied to European customs and clothing. The LP artwork features a monkey wearing an oversized suit with lyrics that add to the ridicule as Kuti remarks:

I know what to wear but my friend don't know
I am not a gentleman like that!
I be African man original

This song was a direct call to Africans to reconnect with their roots and forgo the external influence of the West.

Confusion, an album released by Fela Kuti in 1975, was another prime example of Kuti's forthright commentary.

His signature style was finely honed around the recording of the album. The first song, also named 'Confusion', begins as an abstract departure led by the free flowing improvised drumming of Tony Allen and Kuti playing on electric piano. Lyrically, the haphazard bustle of Lagos markets and traffic is used as a metaphor to satirise the state of Nigeria's oil-rich economy in contrast to the decline of public infrastructure.

With Kuti's popularity rising and the growing disapproval of Nigerian political leaders, home raids from the ruling government were regular occurrences for the megastar. Kuti's performances at well known music venues such as The Africa Shrine and his home 'The Kalakuta Republic' (both across the road from each other) were frequent targets.

'The Kalakuta Republic', which translates to 'Rascal's Republic' in Swahili, was a place Kuti viewed as an independent entity with its own set of rules. Complete with its own court, prison, clinic and barbed wire security system. There Kuti ruled as a traditional chief with his vast entourage of musicians, twenty-seven wives, children and mother all residing there.

The temperature between the state and the showman of the hour would rise in 1977 when Kuti released his seminal album *Zombie*. The album was a direct call to awaken people to the oppressive regimented soldiers Kuti called 'zombies'. The album artwork depicts Kuti in pink silk and small in stature against images of grey metallic helmets.

During the time of the album's release, Kuti's activism increased outside of music. His cultural organisation, the Young African Pioneers (YAP) distributed pamphlets critical of the newly introduced law of whippings for motor offences.

1977 was not only significant due to the release of *Zombie*, but it was also the same year that Nigeria hosted the Black

Arts Festival, FESTAC in Lagos and Kaduna. FESTAC would appear to be a rare celebration of Black culture in Africa. However, due to concerns over the government's extortionate spending and suspected corruption surrounding the festival, many significant cultural makers, such as Kuti, his cousin Wole Soyinka and filmmaker Ola Balohun, dropped out.

During the festival's programming, Kuti performed every night at his venue, The Africa Shrine, attracting international musicians including Stevie Wonder, Sun Ra, Osibisa and South African jazz musician Hugh Masekela. In an essay by Uchenna Ikonne for the *Red Bull Music Academy*, Chyke Madu of Afro-rock band The Funkees states: 'What Fela was doing at The Shrine was more exciting and more raw than any of the other programs. So everybody started to go there instead… the government didn't like that.'

A week after the festival concluded and the international press had returned home, the military swooped on 'the Kalakuta Republic' on 18 February 1977. What would occur on the site would be horriyfing, with around 1,000 soldiers stripping and abusing men as well as raping the female residents. Kuti himself was badly beaten, sustaining a fractured skull and many broken bones. His dear mother was thrown from a second storey window, fracturing her leg and later dying from her injuries on 13 April 1978. A fire was also set, with troops preventing the fire brigade from entering the compound. The fire would take with it all of the Africa 70 frontman's mastertapes, equipment, recording studio and even Kuti's brother's free medical clinic.

Surprisingly, the tragic event did not quell Fela Kuti, in fact, it worked to fuel him even further. In 1978, Kuti spent a brief period of time in Ghana and by 1983, his mother's death and the Kalakuta tragedy served as the catalyst for another band name change, this time to Egypt 80, at the start of a new decade. The change in name reflected the idea that Egyptian civilization and history are African and must be claimed as such. Tensions between Kuti and General Olusegun Obasanjo, the head of state in Nigeria continued to increase.

'Unknown Soldier', released in 1979 by Kuti, was a direct response to Obasanjo's claim that Fela's mother had been thrown out of the window by an 'unknown soldier'. The track reflects on the official enquiry, which announced the army was innocent of burning down 'the Kalakuta Republic'. The artwork, much like the song, oozes boldness. It displays a collage of contradicting headlines about the Kalakuta incident. Within the song itself, Fela hums in midway through the 30-minute melody, and he painfully laments the tragic events that occured. A memorable section of the song is his speech, which breaks the musical pattern with his voice sounding as though he is on the verge of crying:

Them throw my mama
Out of from window
Them kill my mama

The song 'Coffin for Head of State' released in 1981 was a sequel to 'Unknown Soldier'. In this song, Kuti describes the walk to Obasanjo's residence at the Dodan Army Barracks. The song served as a critique of religion from colonial powers, which Kuti believed subjugated Africans. This dichotomy of Africanness and Westernness would be a recurrent theme in his music.

On 30th September 1979, Kuti along with members of his own family and the YAP organisation marched to leave a mock coffin outside the barracks to symbolise his mother's death at the hands of the military.

Kuti's dedication to speaking truth to power was another

recurring theme in his music. Kuti would look outside of Nigeria and address other oppressive regimes in his 1989 album *Beasts of No Nation*, where he condemned the apartheid in South Africa and other world leaders, including Britain's Thatcher and America's Reagan.

The 1990s would see a dramatic decline in Kuti's musical offerings caused by the deterioration of his health. Fela Kuti died in 1997 after a long battle with AIDS, and his funeral in Lagos was filled with the spirit of the people he gave a voice to, with over 5 million people attending.

Fela Kuti was an artist that superseded a specific sound or genre. To many he was a phenomenal musician who carved out a new movement, to others he was an activist who fought for Nigerians and the plight of Africans globally. Kuti's legacy is that of a pioneer who was able to use his generational privilege to change the perception of Africa. With Africa at the heart of Kuti's Afrobeat, West African music was pushed to the masses in unimaginable ways. Today Kuti's Afrobeat has led to a younger pop hybrid that continues to push African music around the world and a generation of African musicians who herald Kuti as the start of it all

3

BURGER HIGHLIFE—
GHANA TO GERMANY

When it comes to genres of the 20th century, high-life music was one of the world's most important. Simply put, highlife is dance music with traditional West African roots. The genre blends these West African sonics with Western elements via jazz, calypso and brass instruments from the marching bands of the British Empire. In the book *African Pop Roots*, writer John Collins notes Ghana as the recognised birthplace of highlife but distinguishes the genre into two derivatives, noting, 'dance bands like E.T. Mensah's Tempos and the Ramblers play[ed] highlife with a jazz and calypso touch and the guitar bands play[ed] electrified Palm-Wine music whose audience [were] in rural areas and among the city poor.' The former style evolved in urban settings, particularly the nightclubs and ballrooms in the Ghanaian capital Accra, where the music was primarily played to wealthy audiences. Interestingly, it would be because of the rich and powerful demographic that the genre would be called highlife. The genre would become central to Ghanaian identity. During the fight for Ghanaian independence, highlife became closely linked with the liberation movement with future Ghanaian President Kwame Nkrumah proclaiming it as 'Ghana's national music'. Highlife bands, including E.T. Mensah & The Tempos, would accompany Nkrumah during his tour of African countries to promote his Pan-Africanist movement.

Post Ghanaian independence, Nkrumah set up the Arts Council of Ghana Law. Its mission was to protect, stimulate and improve the nation's cultural expressions and limit foreign influence on music. In 1961, the Arts Council, in an attempt to hinder the dominance of foreign music in Ghana, would encourage dance bands to infuse highlife with traditional dance and rhythms. With this official mandate, fellow musicians, including E.K. Nyame, Kwaa Mensah and Broadway Band, recorded praise songs for the Ghanaian leader and the country. In his academic paper, 'Popular Performance and Culture', writer John Collins further reflects on the influence of Nkrumah in spreading highlife as a global sound, '[he] was so keen on developing Ghana's home-grown highlife music that he set up training programs for its practitioners home and abroad. He gave scholarships to the up and coming dance band artists, Teddy Osei [who would become the band leader of legendary Afro-rock band Osibisa], Eddie Quansah and Ebo Taylor, to study music in London.' The genre of highlife, though originally a genre for the upper class, morphed into a joyous genre that simultaneously captured the political sentiment in Ghana's halcyon days of independence during the late 1950s and early 1960s.

Following the coup d'etat that removed Kwame Nkrumah as the president of Ghana in 1966, there was a new shift in the political discourse of the nation. The self-sufficiency and Pan-African ideals which held the West African country together soon dissipated.

Subsequent military regimes in Ghana, including the

National Liberation Council (1966–1969), the Supreme Military Council (SMC1) under Ignatius Kutu Acheampong (1975–1979), the Supreme Military Council (SMC11) led by General Fred Akuffo (1978–1979), the Armed Forces Revolutionary Council (AFRC) under Flt Lt Jerry John Rawlings (June 4th 1979–September 24th 1979) and Provisional National Defence Council (1981–1993) under Flt Lt Jerry John Rawlings, would impact the burgeoning highlife scene over the next three decades.

The new military government under Lt Jerry Rawlings and the PNDC (Provisional National Defense Council), which came to power in 1982, curtailed the country's growing musical exports with the implementation of night-time curfews and a 160% tax on imported musical instruments.

Under the new government, the heavily militarised country morphed into a nation where critical thought in the press and entertainment industry was banned. The impact of this on the music scene in Ghana was huge. Rawlings and the PNDC military government worked to stifle the nightlife and music scene as a means of subordinating the secular messaging of highlife. Consequently, artists that remained in Ghana moved into the Pentecostal churches for employment, causing an increase in congregations throughout Ghana in the late 1970s. This would in turn lead to a dramatic rise in Ghanaian and Nigerian gospel music and by the late 80s gospel music accounted for more than half of music airplay in Ghana.

The developments in Ghanaian identity would not end there. Ghanaian identity would be reimagined in another way due to a new change—migration. Travelling abroad from Ghana was once closely associated with the upper-middle classes, who had the cultural capital to move fluidly across countries. Travel in this respect was often aligned with attaining a higher education in prestigious universities abroad. However, Ghana was now struggling with rising unemployment and a famine. This, paired with the relaxation of immigration laws in Germany, saw many Ghanaians, primarily musicians, across social classes move to the European continent. In the 1960s and 1970s, most of the Ghanaian migrants who located to Germany were education migrants who took advantage of lower tuition fees and better opportunities to receive scholarships and gain employment whilst studying. Many Ghanaian refugees also sought asylum due to the ongoing political violence in Ghana. Today, Ghanaians in Germany form the second largest of the country's diaspora population in Europe, after the UK.

This wave of Ghanaian immigrants would firmly cement their presence in Germany. Equipped with highlife as their musical reference, Ghanaian musicians who migrated to Germany, would encounter new technology via drum machines and synthesizers in the homeland of electronic music. It wouldn't be long before these resourceful artists recreated the Ghanaian sounds by using tools from their new German home. Their traditional polyrhythms would ingeniously morph into an analogue amalgamation of big band and guitar highlife, Black funk and disco sensibilities to create a new hybrid genre known as 'Burger highlife'.

The term is a double entendre with Burger, deriving and pinpointing the location of Hamburg—the second largest city in Germany, which also has the largest Ghanaian community in the country. 'Burger' (in this case pronounced bor-ga) is also a Ghanaian slang word used to describe the new cosmopolitan being who leaves Ghana and returns with a new way of dressing or speaking. 'Burger' is emblematic of a mindset and a commonly held fallacy of migration, where owning new commodities such as clothes and technology equates to social and financial advancement. The reality of migration in this case, and most cases, is, of course, very different.

From a musical perspective, Burger highlife is an embodiment of the creative gains of cross-cultural exchanges between Africa and Europe, a facet that has become a long standing feature in the development of music from Africa.

George Darko is credited with inventing Burger highlife in 1983 with the release of the *Friends* LP. The six-track album had a positive impact within Europe before doing well back home in Ghana. The title track 'Friends' is a mix of The Police-esque rocksteady reggae fused with the wonderful vocals of lead singer Lee Dodou. Alongside the other songs 'Capital Punishment', 'Fantasy' and 'Night Train'. The LP would go down well in Ghanaian musical circles, but it would be the last two songs that would set the foundations for the modern marinations of highlife. The penultimate song titled 'Akoo Te Brofo' (The Parrot Understands English in Akan) was the LP's breakout song. The song would be highly influential, replete with superb storytelling which vividly documented life for the diaspora. At just over nine minutes long, Darko's 'Akoo Te Brofo' opens with a galactic crash landing of keys. Darko's lyrics in 'Akoo Te Brofo' weave through his own wisdom blended with African proverbs and symbols reflecting on moving abroad but with the important realisation that no matter what, one can always return home.

The life of Ghanaian migrants like Darko depended heavily on being agile and resourceful—an ideal that represented the 'Burger Lifestyle'. Darko would acknowledge the early shift in sound he was responsible for, stating, 'it is necessary for me to utilize the indigenous Yaa Amponsah style of picking the strings,' in an interview with Florian Carl. 'The drums and bass can be made to play anything, but the guitar and vocals must always bring out the highlife feel.'

The final song on Darko's LP is called 'Medo Menuanom (I love my people)'. The song would continue the modern highlife sonic filled with the ingredients of a funky bass groove with honky tonk piano riffs and Dodou leading from the front on vocals.

John Duke for *the West Africa issue* in 1988 wrote about Darko's musical creation where he explainied it as 'a middle ground for Europeans—giving them the kind of music they are familiar with and at the same time introduce them to the originality and the scope of highlife. Afro-fusion, as Darko calls it, was the result.' Another key factor, which will be explored later in this chapter, is the incubation of the Burger highlife sound in the recording studios of Berlin and Koln (Cologne) and how their owners provided a welcoming space for talented Ghanaian musicians.

Jewel Ackah, Alfred Benjamin Crentsil (A.B Crentsil) and Pat Thomas were widely known as the 'big three' contemporary Ghanaian vocalists and bandleaders during the 1970s. They would serve full musical apprenticeships in innumerable bands that would become pivotal to the evolution of the sound before travelling to the West. Alfred Benjamin Crentsil was leader of popular 70s highlife band The Sweet Talks. The group were the house band of The Talk of the Town Hotel in Tema, Ghana.

In the 1960s, Ghanaians started to migrate to Canada, and in particular, Toronto, where the majority of Ghanaian migrants would settle and build a community. Crenstil would arrive in Toronto in 1985 and would release the *Toronto By Night* LP with his Ahenfo band, a fresh batch of live musicians who would support him on stage and record in studio with him.

The LP featured 5 songs. The final song titled 'I Go Pay You Tomorrow', is a melodious classic filled with trumpet brass and the metronomic cowbell. Crenstil sang in Pidgin English, discussing the use of alcohol to mask the difficulty of survival abroad, relatable to those who struggled to settle away from home.

Jewel Ackah arrived in Toronto in the late 1980s, shortly after Crenstil. In 1989, he released his LP *Me Dear*, recorded at the Oketeke Studios in Canada with master guitarist Alfred Bannerman playing throughout the album.

Pat Thomas arrived in Toronto in 1987 and his LP *Sika Ye Mogya* would be released in 1991. Thomas's LP was recorded at the same Oketeke Studios in Canada as Jewel Ackah. It included the classic title track 'Sika Ye Mogya' (meaning 'money is blood' in the Akan language). 'Sika Ye Mogya' begins with gentle Spanish guitar riffs over programmed drums and synth horns. The track is akin to American poet and musician Gil Scott Heron's metaphorical use of alcohol and its effects on society in his famed song 'The Bottle'. In this instance, Thomas repeats the choral refrain aligning money as a person in the Akan language and Twi dialect in the phrase 'sika ye nipa ampaara' (money is really human).

He sings about a man who is the breadwinner and as a result is chosen to resolve family disputes. Thomas further croons over money's effect on relationships and happiness concluding that with money comes both love and joy.

Thomas's import of African proverbs and tales of diaspora life provided a needed perspective on what life as a migrant was like.

It is now the mid-1980s. On the other side of the Atlantic, back in Germany, Burger highlife is in full swing. Events involving Ghanaian artists and bands are growing throughout the major regions in Germany as Ghanaian communities and curious revellers from the host country are lapping up the Burger sounds.

The Burger highlife experience peaked with an artist called Charles Amoah. Amoah, born and raised in Ghana, came to Germany in the late 1970s. Beginning his German experience in 1979 with German pop band Kamela, Amoah would go on to start his Burger highlife mission with his debut album release *Sweet Vibration* in 1984. The title song was intentionally sung in English for broader global appeal. Subsequent singles Shake Your Body To The Beat and Scratch My Back would receive further popularity across Europe.

Amoah would, however, return to singing in the Akan language the following year when he released his LP *Fre Me (Call Me)* in 1985.

The aforementioned George Darko was on lead guitar alongside Bob Fiscan on the keys. The back cover art of the LP showed Charles Amoah chilling in front of a public water feature doing up his imaginary cufflinks like your favourite Instagram model, with his love interest gazing longingly in the background.

The LP went down a storm with local Germans and was similarly popular among members of the Ghanaian community in Europe and North America.

By the late 80s, Charles Amoah had proved he was a main contender for the Burger highlife crown, if there ever was such a thing, but it was in 1987 when his true genius came to be. Recorded in Dusseldorf at Skyline Studios with influential Burger highlife figures Bodo Staiger and Peter Krick behind the scenes, *Ɛyɛ Ɔdɔ Asɛm* (Akan for it's a love story) would be

Amoah's third, and arguably most impactful, LP. Released on his own independent label Cage Records in 1987, the album cover provides poignant reflection on Amoah as an artist and father living in Germany.

The first song of the LP would show Amoah warble proudly in Twi dialect sounding confident in his dual identity. Now settled in Europe, Amoah would assertively sing about love. The instrumental backdrop is funk-laden with heavy electric influence hybridized with gospel drums and light chords.

The album was infectious, enticing its listeners with its futuristic sounds galvanised by Moog synths and familiar rhythms played on electronic drum machines all produced by Amoah himself. The sonic addictiveness would become particularly apparent on the song 'Sesa Wo Suban' (Akan for change your style). The 7-minute-and-24 second song is a direct call to dance and embrace your individuality in a new environment. The sentiment of the song would contrast the frequently explored challenges of migrant life.

Burger highlife was a template of electronica which refused to sound generic and lifeless, instead it was infused with a different foundation, one that was inherently African.

At his height, Charles Amoah, backed by a supportive Ghanaian community in Europe and America, played alongside the Germany-based Black disco group Boney M. at a music gala event in Dusseldorf, this was in the same year *3y3 Odo As3m* was released as the first record on his label.

Highlife presented Ghanaians with a reinvention of identity abroad but not without help. It is often the case that musicians in new climes find hospitable facilitators that selflessly aid their efforts in exploring their experience of Western society. In 1980s London, an advert in Loot magazine was making the rounds, offering the services of the Linn Drum, a seminal electro drum machine imitating percussive sounds. The Linn

Drum was used on global hits, such as A-Ha's 'Take On Me' and Harold Faltermeyer's 'Axel F', also known as the Beverly Hills Cop Theme tune or Crazy Frog if you're of a certain age. A Ghanaian-born artist would somehow come across this advert and respond. Unbeknownst to anyone at the time, this would be the start of a creative journey which would vibrate across the West African diaspora.

'This guy rang me up, "yeah I wanna rent your machine," and I said, "Yeah cool it would be this much," and he said, "but I don't know how to programme it,"' says musician Dave Yowell also known as Sultan Makende. The guy Dave Yowell spoke to was the late Jonathan Opoku, better known as Jon K, a Ghanaian musician and artist who was looking to experiment with cutting-edge technology for a project he was working on for highlife O.G. Pat Thomas.

Now based in Salvador, Brazil, a city where 80% of its residents are of African heritage, I speak to Yowell via Skype, where he reminisces on the good old days.

Born and raised in Kenya but of British heritage, Yowell was influenced by a range of sounds from psychedelic rock, funk to soul. Yet, it was his fascination with the groove of African, Arabian and Indian music that would allow him to compose a number of projects as a musician and engineer for four decades.

So, back to the 1980s, where Yowell had just received the phone call from Jon K. Yowell agreed to help Jon with programming the drum machine, as well as offering him his own recording studio to record at. This was the start of a fruitful musical relationship, one that would lead to highlife star Pat Thomas's project being completed at Yowell's North London base, Sultan Sound in Kilburn. Formerly an abandoned terraced house, Yowell would get a tipoff from a fellow musician who worked for a housing association about this new available space. Yowell, not willing to let a good opportunity go by, would take the space as his own. He would proceed to renovate the ground floor into a studio, upgrading it with top-end equipment and acoustic treatments to ensure a crisp sounding room for recording.

When speaking about the advancement in technology and how it affected software, Yowell stated that there was, 'no digital in those days at the beginning,' however, he went on to explain, 'as the digital revolution came along and I brought the first computers that could run... you could start recording digitally ... the space was quite small, but it had a control room and live room.'

Yowell's effort led to the Kilburn studio becoming a central point of activity for a number of established and up-and-coming African artists travelling from Africa as well as those already in the UK. Notable albums recorded at Sultan Sound included Jon K's *Adowa* and Thomas Frimpong's *Menenamu*. Ben Brako's *Baya*, released in 1987, is arguably the most well known and acclaimed production to emerge from Sultan Sound. Yowell, who played bass on the album, witnessed its impact first-hand whilst travelling in Ghana. 'It was a beat fusion with a lot of electronic back stuff in it. [Ben Brako's] compositions were so simple and so catchy that's why he was so successful.' Yowell explains with admirable nostalgia, 'I remember being in Accra and pulling into a petrol station as I was on my way to a city in the North [of Ghana] with a friend and we refilled. They had this sound system playing Ben Brako and I said, "hey I know that music, I recorded it in London."'

Ben Brako's love for re-imagining percussive grooves and ensuring the continuity of polyrhythms from Africa across the Atlantic was retained even with the use of electronic instruments.

Yowell explains, 'to be honest there were some formulas

really which since I started working at the beginning with Jon K, I just kept using like, "This is the standard BPM we should be working at and the swing has to be this way or that way." We would get there quickly and make creative templates of how to get there.' It's a work pattern that Yowell uses to this day, collaborating with Brazilian artists in his new location, which he likens to Ghana because of the good weather, culture and the kind nature of the people. In a digital age where the liner notes on CD sleeves are forgotten about it is easy for those behind the scenes to slip through the cracks. In Yowell's case, his story aids in connecting the dots between the past and present when it comes to Afrobeats.

During a nocturnal break from the mid-quarantine madness, I made a detour into the world of TV shows to detach myself from being productive (writing this book). I found a TV series remake of High Fidelity. Originally a book, with it's story based in London. The High Fidelity (2020) . The show follows record store owner and erudite music aficionado Rob played by Zoe Kravitz. During the opening scenes of the third episode, I heard a familiar sweet tone sung in the Twi dialect.

The tune in question was called 'Akwankwa' (Akan for duke) by highlife musician Lee Dodou. After watching the episode, I found Dodou's Bandcamp profile and sent him an email, expecting to never hear back. To my surprise, I received a prompt response that included a German mobile number followed by copious thumbs up emojis. So, I dialed the number and waited as it rang. A warm uncle greeted me from his Berlin home and almost instantly he began to open up, smiling at the memories of 'those days'.

An early purveyor of the Burger highlife sound, Uncle Lee was born in Kumasi, the cultural capital of the historical Asante Empire in Ghana. From a young age, Uncle Lee was known for being a talented singer at his elementary school based in the area of Asafo, Ghana. Yet as he recalls, it was initially through word of mouth that Lee caught the ear of a famous guitar band in his local neighbourhood of Asokwa. 'The old guys saw my talent and I was lucky at that time as one of the best highlife singers was living in my street. So he came to my home and asked for me and put me on. He brought me to the leader of the band and that was it.' The band in question was the iconic highlife group Yamoah's Band, led by the talented great P.K. Yamoah who would win the high honour of the Musical Merit Award in Ghana decades later. Still an apprentice Dodou was given the nickname 'Small' due to the fact that he was the youngest person around the band. The influence of African-American soul via the records of Otis Redding and Sam Cooke would inspire a young Lee Dodou, who would regularly sit by the hi-fi writing down song lyrics and imitating the past masters. A mutual mentorship would commence with Yamoah teaching Lee Dodou and his instrumentalist peers the fundamentals of the highlife style.

Dodou would have brief stints in multiple bands such as the Ghana Police Dance Band, the Lantics Band, Gyedu Blay Ambolley's band Zantoda MK 3 and his own band Bisa Goma in the mid-70s. It wouldn't be long before the talented Dodou received a call from highlife musician Pat Thomas who was seeking a vocalist for a new band he was forming in Germany. Dodou eager and raring to go, packed up and moved to Berlin in 1979 and, unbeknownst to him, would never leave.

Now in Berlin, Lee Dodou took odd jobs to survive before eventually immersing himself in the music. In 1982, the formation of the Bus Stop Band had begun, this group included guitarist George Darko, keyboardist Bob Fiscian, bassist B.B. Dowuona and our very own Lee Dodou on vocals.

The Bus Stop Band's music would lead to a new highlife

sound. As Dodou recounts his memories with the band to me, he reflects on the massive contribution of keyboardist Bob Fiscian. Remember when I mentioned 'Akoo Te Brofo' by George Darko? Well, it turned out Lee Dodou was there when Fiscian was working on it. 'Before we started to play around we had to put up a demo to give to agents so that we can get promoted as well. We started on 'Akoo Te Brofo', but when we started, that melody is actually from C.K. Mann. George Darko started playing the same guitar melody and Bob [Fiscian] didn't like it as it wasn't interesting for him. He was fed up with that kind of keyboarding in highlife so he stopped the whole practice and said, "guys you can't do it like this."'

Dodou went on to explain, '[Bob Fiscian said] "Why don't we play it like Black Americans would?"'. The story would go that Fiscian would ask the bass player to imitate his piano melody and the rest was history. In Dodou's opinion this became the sound of Borga highlife, 'I believe Bob Fiscian is the main guy [behind it]as he brought [up] the idea and we bought into it'. Influenced by Herbie Hancock's *Headhunters* LP and his own adoption of the Moog synth in particular, Fiscian's fascination with technology, as well as performing with Lionel Richie as his main keyboardist when he toured Germany in the 80s, encouraged other African musicians to approach highlife in new ways.

'Akoo Te Brofo''s crossover success in 1983 was an early example of what could be possible for African artists. It led to icons like Mory Kante of Guinea, Congo's Kanda Bongo Man, Ivory Coast's Alpha Blondy and Benin's Angelique Kidjo, all artists whose music would reach the West without having to assimilate or modify their sound. Interestingly, Angelique Kidjo, who would later become a multi-Grammy Award winning artist, lived in Berlin for a time and attended the Empire Club, a live music spot where the Bus Stop Band played at regularly.

At the height of The Bus Stop band's popularity, they split in the late 80s after bandleader George Darko went back to Ghana. This left Lee Dodou without a group once again. It would take further convincing before Dodou would go forward with a fresh band called Kantata and release the aforementioned hit single 'Akwankwa' from the *Ashiko* LP. A vibrant song that explored the pressure to succeed for family back home whilst being unable to afford one's own ticket back.

For Lee Dodou the song was personal, 'it's a serious thing you know because I had a big fallout with my parents and my father had three wives you know. There was this womanly rivalry between them and my mum was the first one and I was the last born of my mum. This thing [was] ...a kind of pain and my mum did love me you know. Like any mother and son… I wanted to do something for her... My brother was lost in the USA and he refused to come back to Ghana. So, life was quite hard for us so I made a promise to her that I will struggle to make money, take care of her and build her a house.' He adds, 'that's why I made the song because I came and saw that it wasn't easy ...I was talking to [my mum] on that song.'

Still a resident of West Berlin and performing of late with the Polyversal Souls band in the German capital, Lee Dodou's soulful tones are still in demand and are soothing as ever. Lee Dodou, or Uncle Lee as I prefer to address him, is a figure-whose musical curiosity took him to the forefront of Burger highlife and eventually led him to become an important contributor of a rich musical culture.

The location of Sinus Ton Studio in Berlin facilitated a number of releases from George Darko and Lee Dodou in the early epoch of the Burger highlife sound. The studio's manager Bodo Staiger was a German fascinated by the first influx of Ghanaian musicians and their sound. Staiger soon left Sinus Ton Studio and set up his own RheinKlang Studios closer to home in Dusseldorf. Here he would invite a young Charles Kwadwo Fosu better known as Daddy Lumba to record in the mid-1980s. Staiger would be behind the mixing board for a healthy amount of Daddy Lumba's 1992 album 'Playboy's' and would have a hand in recording the famed shoulder skank-inducing record *Aben Wo Ha (It Is Cooked Here)*, released in 1998. This musical relationship would lead the second wave of Burger highlife musicians in the early 90s passing through the studio to record. This included the likes of Nana Tuffour, the Tagoe Sisters, Nana Acheampong, Ofori Amponsah all entering the doors of Staiger's studio in the 80s and 90s. Staiger's impact on Ghanaian music set an unrivaled precedent, creating solo stars who are still revered more than three decades after Burger highlife's inception.

4

HIPLIFE—
FUSION AND CULTURE

Camaraderie in making music is something that flows through the roots of traditional palm wine music.

'What is palm wine music?' I hear you ask. Well, the story goes a little something like this: in the 1920s Portuguese, Spanish and Caribbean sailors whose ships docked at the ports of Freetown (Sierra Leone), Lagos (Nigeria), Accra/Tema (Ghana) and Monrovia (Liberia) lent their guitars and musical style to their African shipmates. The Kru people (an ethnic group indigenous to Liberia), in turn, evolved these guitar melodies with Trinidadian calypso rhythms. Music, however, wasn't the only thing these musicians would bond over—herein enters the wine. Yes, that's right—these guitarists would develop their musical union over palm wine, an alcoholic beverage created from the sap of various species of palm tree, a tree native to Nigeria, Ghana and the Democratic Republic of Congo. The consumption of palm wine had a deep influence on musicians and listeners who enjoyed the sweet beverage whilst listening to the mesmerizing sounds of West African music. The name palm wine music perfectly encapsulates yet another valuable relationship—the link between food, drink and music in African culture.

'There were so many experimental bands... even the government had bands. The excitement of entertainment was right there.' These are the words of Gyedu Blay-Ambolley, who said this to me over a Whatsapp call. Gyedu Blay-Ambolley is an erudite Ghanaian grandfather who played a role in the rise of West African music.

Known as 'The Sekondi Man' due to the fact he was born in the port city of Sekondi-Takoradi, in the western region of Ghana, Blay-Ambolley's reflective words go back to his early upbringing in Ghana. He was raised in a location that was an early port town where European colonialists, including the Portuguese, Dutch and British, set up imposing forts in the 15th century. By the 1960s this base became a focal point where Ghanaian seamen from Kwame Nkrumah's Black Star Line (a state-owned maritime corporate entity used for trade) would bring back jazz records from their travels.

Gyedu Blay-Ambolley was first a drummer, bass player and saxophonist, guided by his friend the legendary Ebo Taylor, who performed with Afrobeat O.G. Fela Kuti during the late 1960s and early 1970s. It was during this time that Blay-Ambolley developed an experimental musical approach that would lay the foundation for the genre that would become known as hiplife in decades to come.

Hiplife, like most African genres and subgenres, is not something that can be truly captured in a single sentence, but at its essence, it is a musical style that amalgamates Ghanaian highlife samples and polyrhythms with the unapologetic bravado of African-American rap and conscious hip hop.

A number of Ghanaian bands would contribute to the development of this new hiplife sound including the seminal Uhuru Dance Band and Stargazers in the late 1960s. However, it was the introduction of the 'Simigwa*-do' sound in 1973 and the release of the *Simigwa* album in 1975 that cemented

---

* The name of a dance originating from Ambolley's home city in a place called Asemensudo

Gyedu Blay-Ambolley's legacy as the godfather of hiplife. The Simigwa album would be released on the influential Essiebons label, a Ghanaian owned record label set up by the late Dick Essilfie-Bondzie

Personifying the playfulness of his early youth, Blay-Ambolley would use his voice to mimic instruments he and fellow friends couldn't afford. In serendipitous form, this phonetic-onomatopoeic approach led him to influence a whole generation to fuse musical styles whilst paying homage to their traditional roots.

During the course of our interview, Blay-Ambolley reiterated the little known fact that he (and not the Sugarhill Gang) recorded the first ever rap record: 'If you go to the *Guinness Book of Records* they say [the first ever commercially recorded rap] was the Sugarhill Gang...but that was around 1978 or 1979. Mine came out in 1973.' Blay-Ambolley believes the art of rap traces back to Ghanaian royalty. He tells me, 'among the queens and kings, we people are linguists. They are [people] who sing praises or speak praises to the King when he is coming. It's totally rap. That fast pace of speaking.' When Blay-Ambolley released his rap song in 1973, the influence of African American artists such as James Brown was taking over the world. James Brown's music in particular resonated with Blay-Ambolley at the height of the Black Power movement in the US. in the early 1970s Hiplife's emergence rather interestingly aligned with rediscovering and asserting one's Black identity.

Hiplife was predominantly versed and recorded in Akan—the most widely used language in Ghana to the present day. It is a genre with origins in hip hop, dancehall and the older sonic sibling of highlife. Talking Drums were among the first groups to rap in the Twi dialect of the Akan language. The Talking Drums duo consisted of Kwaku-T and Abeiku (now known as Jay Ghartey) who released the single 'Aden' (which means why in Akan language) in 1993. The track follows their fluid home-grown lineage via a sample lifted from late Ghanaian musician CK Mann's The 'Aden'. The music video is a simple yet striking affair filmed in black and white with Kwaku and Abeiku dressed in a 90s Brooklyn aesthetic wrapped in an African flavour. The pair switch between traditional Kente* and flipped flat caps mirroring the swag of the golden era boom-bap.

The lyrics are quick to address the deeply flawed Western perception of Africa. In their words, Kwaku-T and Abeiku touch on the tired African tropes of cinematic exoticism, from swinging off vines to living in trees. The existence and popularity of these tropes is something that many from the continent still push back against today.

In the last verse of the song, Abeiku delivers the most poignant prose rapping about a fellow countryman losing his way and becoming a drug dealer in the States. Abeiku laments on the man's predicament and the way in which he has tried to help him by sending him 'back home'.

It is mid-December and I am in the midst of yet another humid daytime trek in Accra. My Uber driver, who was lovely during our drive, attempted to hold me hostage at the end of my journey as his internet connection failed to allow him to complete the trip. Anyway, once the Uber driver used my data to complete the trip, I meet a patient pioneer behind the aforementioned Talking Drums group.

Amidst the incessant hum of cool air ventilation and a wall

---

*   a handwoven Ghanaian textile cloth made out of silk and cotton associated with royalty amongst the Asante ethnic group from Kumasi

filled with paintings of Black leaders, men like Kofi Annan and Malcolm X, a man called Panji Anoff begins telling me about the parallels between hiplife and Afrobeats. 'I don't know if Afrobeats is a term which sits well with me, but I think it's fantastic that everything is finding itself under one umbrella. I hoped this movement would happen with hiplife and I understood that it would need a lot of momentum here in Ghana, but I have to admit I didn't see the Pan-African picture straight away.'

Born Panji Marc Owooh Anoff in London in the 1970s, Panji Anoff was a talented creative from a young age. Anoff would move back to Ghana as a child, it was here that he developed an early relationship with music, playing various instruments. A keen musical observer, Anoff would watch teachers play instruments, which would lead him to recording and producing demos for professional bands at the tender age of 11.

Anoff soon returned to London for university where he balanced working for the BBC as a journalist. The music bug would suck Anoff back in and in the early 1990s he would return as an Artist Manager. It was during this time that Anoff's involvement in developing Ghanaian music and artists would begin, coinciding with the early beginnings of the hiplife scene.

After witnessing the home-grown rise of UK hip hop, Ragga rap and jungle from the mid-1980s Anoff returned to Ghana again, investing money earned from a stint as screenwriter on Channel 4's show *Desmond's* to support hiplife musicians in the mid-1990s.

'At least half of the people who were interested in hiplife at the time, I recorded demos for and I did it all for free even if I was paying for the studio at the time.' Anoff explains further 'I understood the importance of a movement even though I had my own particular interest in the artists I was managing, but I also invested into a broader movement simply because I could afford to.' He also recalls an early trip to America with his group Talking Heads and their influence on a classic Busta Rhymes anthem, 'I took my African hip hop group to New York and Atlanta (in 1995) and sure they made an impact. [They] influenced 'Put Your Hands Where Your Eyes Can See (Busta Rhymes's song)' which is very obviously African music even though it's American hip hop.'

Following this crossover attempt into the American market 25 years too early with hip hop still very much a subculture in the USA, Anoff recognised that back in Ghana if a song was a hit it would immediately be mainstream given that half the population was under 18. After listening to Nigerian group Plantashun Boiz and similar acts who rapped in Pidgen English around the early 2000s, Anoff changed the name of his record label to Pidgen Music paying homage to the unofficial lingua franca of Nigeria. 'The English language has mastered the art of hiding emotions and Pidgen has mastered the art of expressing emotions.', Anoff explained. 'You can see what made the revolution to how artists expressed themselves—it was the use of the Pidgen language. It allowed them to be more aggressive lyrically .They sit much earlier on the beat and also Pidgen is naturally musical.' Anoff gave an example saying, '"Chale where you dey go," that's music already. "Ah dey go come (pa-pa-pa-pa)."' Anoff's insight into the linguistic and musical freedom of Pidgen English rings true today, with African artists often bouncing between English and Pidgen English in their music .

❀❀❀

In the book *Hiplife In Ghana*, writer Halifu Osumare speaks to Ghanaian artist Obour, who marks out the distinct phases that created hiplife :

> **Phase 1:** *Strictly hip hop rhythm with a local dialect (beginning era of Reggie Rockstone) [One of the early pioneers of hiplife who played a pivotal role in the development of the subgenre since 1994)*

> **Phase 2:** *hip hop mixed with local beats and local dialect (First gen hiplife)*

> **Phase 3:** *Extremely traditional rhythms with traditional lyrics on it which is highlife by production and instrumentation, with twi or any other local dialect (Second Generation hiplife)*

> **Phase 4:** *English on the local beat*

> **Phase 5:** *Gradually going back to hip hop beat with a fusion of hip hop, English language and minor Twi (Current Third Gen hiplife & hip hop)*

Reggie Rockstone is a UK born Ghanaian rapper who is widely heralded as the 'Godfather of hiplife'. Born Reginald Osei in London in 1964 seven years after Ghana's independence, he was taken back to the motherland as a child before moving to the United States as a young adult in the 1980s. Before returning to Ghana as an adult, Reggie would be part of UK based hip hop group Party Á La Mazon aka PLZ in the early '90s . He would even open concerts for hip hop stars like Pete Rock and CL Smooth. However, a chance encounter with one members of the Jungle Brothers who remarked about a forthcoming trip to Africa would be the true turning point for Rockstone's musical trajectory. He returned to Ghana for the first time in years in 1994 for PANAFEST, a cultural event held in Ghana every two years. Known for spearheading one of Ghana's original musical genres, Rockstone would go on to release six studio albums, winning the Kora award (music awards given for musical achievement in Sub-Saharan Africa) for Best Music Video in 2004 for Fa Me Boni Kye Me (feat KK Fosu). Rockstone would go on to collaborate with the likes of 2Face (2Baba), Beenie Man, Wyclef Jean and Idris Elba. Today Rockstone is a successful entrepreneur and still releases music. The dreadlocked Rockstone in both his story and artistry represents the dual identity of Ghana's musical past and present.

In a CNN documentary on hiplife released in 2015, Reggie Rockstone references the three B's of *'Brooklyn, Brixton and Bukom'* as important Black neighbourhoods that influenced him on his musical and personal journey in the diaspora. Rockstone's three B's statement is an interesting one as the locations mentioned represent the lines of the triangular slave trade connecting those of African descent.

Crucially for Rockstone, his geographical journey from the UK to America in the 80s would mean he would become uniquely exposed to the rise of rap and hip hop in both locations.

Rockstone's verve for the hustle and creative excellence was in a similar vein to that of his late father, Ricci. Ricci, also known as Saint Ossei, was a renowned Ghanaian fashion designer rumoured to be the creator of patched jeans in 1970. His eye was responsible for the world class packaging on Rockstone's first album *Makaa Maka,* which would influence a new generation's creative approach to artwork, and he also served as executive producer on the album. Interestingly in his younger days Ricci showed so much promise that he caught the eye of Ghana's first President Kwame Nkrumah, who nurtured his early creativity and placed him on a school scholarship. A symbolic gesture which championed Black excellence with a vision for the future of the young nation. This in turn would allow his son Reggie to take a privileged position due to his father's education and creative exploits.

Rockstone's return to Ghana in 1994 finally saw him 'feel back home' and culminated in the release of his debut LP *Makaa Maka* (which translates from the Akan language as I said it, because I said it in English) in 1997. The LP introduced a blend of R&B, hip hop with highlife sensibilities to a new audience in the West. However, it would be his second LP release in 1998 called *Me Na Me Kae*, which translates to, 'I was the one who said it' that would cement him as an icon of hiplife . Both album names were influenced by Rockstone's love of New York, specifically hip hop group EPMD whose use of the word 'business' in every title of the one of their albums inspired Reggie. The LP was released on his own independent label, Kassa Records and its release would strengthen Rockstone's connection to the past masters of highlife with tracks such as 'Keep Your Eyes On The Road', 'Ya Bounce Visa' and 'Eye Mode Anaa'.

Sampling seminal songs such as Ghanaian highlife singer Alhaji K Frimpong's single 'Kyenkyen Bi Adi Mawu' and Fela Kuti's 'Shakara', Rockstone's fluid flow was equally organic with clarity in English, Asante Twi and local Pidgin to appease an elder generation who initially frowned upon this new hip hop influenced sound.

Lord Kenya was another contemporary of Rockstone who was also in the hiplife scene. Born and raised in Kumasi, Ghana in 1978, Lord Kenya was born Abraham Philip Akpor Kojo and would, like Rockstone, become known for his combination of enticing rapping in both Akan and English. He first gained popularity after featuring on the late 90s single 'Kokooko' by the late Daasebre Gyamenah, a well known Ghanaian highlife musician.

Lord Kenya's rap verse on 'Kokooko' was memorable and addictive. It arrives in perfect timing at around the 4-minute-and-40-second mark of the 6-and-a-half-minute song. The song has a meandering drum loop akin to Brandy's late 90s classic 'U Don't Know Me (Like U Used To)'. Following over 4 minutes of Daasebre Gyamenah's gentle two-step inducing vocals, Lord Kenya's shouty and striking entrance into the song was somehow the perfect fit. He remarks on his courtship of a potential love interest by admiring her voice and figure, and the trouble that could ensue if he pursues a relationship with her. Notable mentions of Lord Kenya's discography, who has since become a born-again evangelist, include his single 'Sika Baa' (Golddigger) released in 2000. The song explored themes of money, love and survival communicating in classic folk song fashion. At the time of its release it resonated with a growing youth population at home and abroad providing real social commentary on the reality of life within Ghana. His perspective on the song most likely came from his experiences with groupies as his level of fame increased.

Lord Kenya would go on to win the Ghanaian hiplife of the Year Award in 2001 at the Ghana Music Awards among other accolades for his musical contributions. Like Rockstone, Lord Kenya had a relatively middle-class upbringing. In both of their cases, Rockstone and Lord Kenya's exposure and education enabled them to effectively articulate and speak on issues affecting a majority of Ghanaians in Ghana and abroad.

Hiplife, like many subgenres which emerged post-highlife, was derided by the older generation. The disapproval of new cultural expressions by those that came before seems to be a natural part of new and emerging cultures. In conservative Ghana, led by its own colonial import of the church, the 'older generation' found flaws in hiplife's overt and unapologetic form, finding it both outlandish and disrespectful. Hiplife accidentally found itself in competition with religion when it came to informing the morals and values of a new generation. Hiplife reflects a constant conversation between 'the traditional' and 'the contemporary', articulating what it means to be African, forever in transit.

One figure who was an anomaly amidst the machismo-filled hiplife scene was a musician called Mzbel, born Belinda Nana Ekua Amoah. The first lady of the genre with echoes of Lil Kim and Da Brat, her popular hit '16 Years' addresses sexual abuse and harassment in a domestic setting. Her approach was rare and bold as she chose to engage with topics that were considered taboo. In her track she would sing, 'I be 16 years, I go dey be like this o/If you touch my thing o, I go tell Poppy o,' over a traditional woodwind rhythm. The message warns young girls and women to be extra vigilant of men who seek to take advantage of them. Mzbel's Wikipedia entry describes her as an artist known for 'controversial traits' .To many, particularly those of the older generation who were fearful of hiplife and its fruits, this Wikipedia entry probably rings true, however, Mzbel was more than a 'controversial' act, she was in fact trailblazing and necessary. Mzbel was a woman in a highly traditional environment where women were deemed rude or ungrateful for speaking such truths but she refused to bend. Her songs provide a deeper assessment of the wider society in Ghana in relation to the safety and freedom of women.

Released in 1999, Obrafour's debut LP *Pae Mu Ka* (which translates to, 'say it as it is') is still largely recognised as the best hiplife album to come from Ghana, winning three awards including the coveted rapper of The Year accolade at the Ghana Music Awards in 2000.

Born Michael Elliot Kwabena Okyere-Darko, Obrafour also known as 'The Rap Executioner', exploded onto the scene in 1999 and hiplife would never be the same again. Obrafour's 10 track debut album featured some of the most memorable tracks that continue to be played far and wide in Ghanaian households and hall parties alike. The sixth song on the album, named *Yaanom*, opens with a woman singing in traditional hymn chimes before the 'rap sofo' (pastor (in Akan language) takes over atop programmed drums asking people to gather before his storytelling commences. *Yaanom* would become a cult favourite intergenerationally and the musicality of the song spoke to the older generation reminding them of traditional customs and educating the younger population of their history.

Another key figure behind this success and the growth of the early hiplife movement was music producer Hammer of the Last Two. Born Edward Nana Poku Osei in 1976, he assumed the alter-ego after previously being part of a production duo with fellow producer Way Deep called The Last Two, meaning the only two left to put Ghana on the world map musically. Hammer of the Last Two would be heavily influential in steering the sound of Obrafour's LP *Pae Mu Ka*, Hammer and co-producer Way Deep would craft the music of Obrafour's seminal LP guided by their desire to represent Ghana globally. Hammer's musical vision was to show the richness of the other Ghanaian dialects that were not centered around the Southern majority who spoke the Akan language and Twi dialect. Hammer would go on to connect with various artists across the country using music as a medium to showcase the diversity in Ghanaian dialogue.

TEMA

The geographical journey of hiplife is another important element in the genre's development. Every genre has the central location where it all began before it develops within other locations. Hip hop music has New York and Grime music has London, Jazz music has New Orleans and the list goes on. In the case of hiplife, its central location is Tema, a city in Ghana. Tema plays an important part in the early wave of hiplife, but before I go into how, let me explain why.

Tema is a coastal city located 16 miles east of the capital Accra. It was commissioned by Ghana's first President Kwame Nkrumah, who developed the site from a small fishing village into an important trading centre which is now Ghana's largest seaport. Nicknamed the 'Harbour City'. Tema's access to imported food and cultural markers such as music brought back from seamen introduced the locals of Tema to an early taste of what Western culture had to offer. This interaction would lead to the fusion of the English language, Ghanaian culture and religion, which would eventually breed hiplife.

Tema handles 80% of Ghana's imports and exports trading goods to fellow landlocked countries like Mali, Burkina Faso and Niger. This trading background informs the hustler mentality and hard-working aura of the population that live in the coastal city.

Tema is the birthplace of influential Ghanaian musicians R2Bees and rapper Sarkodie. The former are a seminal hiplife duo composed of Paeda (Faisal Hakeem) and Mugeez (Rashid Mugeez), who have been performing together since school in rap contests. The pair, known for their feelgood aura and determined mentality chose the name R2Bees, which stands for Refuse 2 Be Broke. R2Bees would develop a playful musical style that would incorporate English, Twi and groovy new age melodies. Their first musical release would be in August 2008 and their discography would quickly develop and cement them as one of the most influential hiplife artists to come out of the 2000s. The pair would collaborate with artist Wande Coal on one of their early popular Afro-pop songs 'Kiss Your Hand' released in 2009. Coal's appearance on the song would be the start of the duo regularly collaborating with Nigerian artists such as Wizkid and Davido.

Another regular collaborator of R2Bees was Ghanaian rapper Sarkodie, who took the path to wider stardom via a rap competition on Ghanaian radio station Adom FM. Born Michael Owusu Addo in 1988, Sarkodie is regularly noted as one of Africa's finest rappers. Known for his hypnotic rhythmic rapping ability and clear cadence—Sarkodie's rapping style is both unapologetically Ghanaian and palatable to Western audiences. He seamlessly blends Akan and Americanised English. It is this wide ranging musical combination that means he is often seen as one of modern Africa's most versatile mainstream acts.

Sarkodie, like many great artists is also known for his onomatopoeic ad-libs, his most notable ones being 'What Else' and perhaps my favourite 'pim-pim-dee-poor-pee-dee' all regularly supported by his cry of, 'you know dat money no be problem'.

Another notable mention in the hiplife lineage is Ghanaian group VVIP, an acronym for Vision In Progress (initially the group's name was VIP). Hailing from Nima, an informal neighbourhood in the capital Accra, Nima translates to 'Nii's Town' in Ga and has a literal meaning of 'city of the King'. The group was formed in 1997 and released their first three albums Bibi Baa O, Ye De Aba and Lumbe Lumbe Lumbe in 1998, 2000, and 2001 respectively. However, it wasn't until the release of their fourth album *Ahomka Womu* in 2003 that the hiplife group conquered the Ghana music charts. The single, which shared the same name as the album title, would be their biggest hit to date. 'Ahomka Wo Mu' sat at number one on the Ghanaian charts for over 20 weeks and would go on to win innumerable awards, including Song of the Year at The Ghana Music Awards in 2004. The group won the Most Popular Artiste of the Year Award at the Nigeria Music Awards in 2005. This further highlighted their popularity outside of their homeland and at the height of their fame, the group embarked on a European tour in 2007.

The population of Nima is distinct in its makeup with a rare blend of ethnic groups in Hausa, Akan and Ga. Nima has an important influence on original VIP members Zeal (formerly known as Lazy), Prodigal and Promzy. In *The Hiplife in Ghana* book released in 2013, Lazy speaks about the group's pride in Nima's diversity, 'Promzy was rapping in Twi. I was rapping in Hausa. Everybody was rapping in English too at the same time'. The multilingual approach of VIP and more broadly of Nima itself is a testament to the inclusive representation of hiplife.

The addition of Reggie Rockstone in 2013 happened after group member Promzy exited VIP. This change led to the group changing their name from VIP to VVIP. The group may not be as active in their heyday, but VVIP's impact was huge and continues to inspire many Ghanaian artists today.

One artist who for me is emblematic of the future of hiplife is Pure Akan. Born Bernard Nana Yaw Appiah, his debut album *Onipa Akoma (The Heart of Man)* released in 2017 received great reviews.

Popular track 'Mi Sika Aduro' is a new age sonic sibling

to Pat Thomas' Sika Ya Mogya, which spoke about migrating abroad and the finacial challenges that come with that, particularly when you have family to provide for. Pure Akan is still relatively young, yet the level of precision and detail in his music and fashion is reflective of a modern day griot.

Writer Jesse Shipley, in a 2013 interview with *Afropop Worldwide*, notes a pivotal political moment in Ghana which aided the 'development of hiplife'. Ghana's constitution changed in 1992 when hiplife was still very much in its infancy, the country returned to democratic rule after decades of military power in the 1970s and 1980s. It was a constitution which mandated the privatization of media, guaranteeing the independence of media and making any form of censorship unconstitutional. The consequence of this was a rise in the private ownership of TV and radio stations. This fostered a rebirth in local talent, with new platforms for their creativity to be recognised without fear of state reprisal.

The Ghanaian Broadcasting Corporation was renamed in 1957 and during its long history GBC has been a tool of nation building and education. It also served as an instrument of propaganda and control. This in turn saw the GBC play a major role in carving out a national identity throughout the country's colonial and post-colonial society. Following the country's fourth attempt at a republican democratic government since independence, the 1992 constitution change took a further two years to complete privatisation of radio broadcasting . The privatisation of the industry would run alongside the establishment of pirate FM station 'Radio Eye' in Accra in May 1994. However, after only 24 hours of broadcasting, state security shut down the station. This action led to riots and protests in the capital of Ghana. It wouldn't be until 1995 that the Ghana Frequency Registration and Control Board (GFRCB) put the call out for applicants to operate broadcasting services independent of the state-owned Ghana Broadcasting Corporation. The first frequencies were assigned in July 1995 for ten commercial radio stations to operate in the Ghanaian cities of Accra, Kumasi and Sekondi-Takoradi.

This created a wider approach to what is known as broadcast pluralism. It is a concept that embraces a number of aspects, such as diversity of ownership, variety in the sources of information and in the range of contents available in the different member states. This enabled a broader scope for local dialects to be used in news broadcasts and music. As a result this provided opportunity for home-grown artists in developing scenes.

Hiplife created a Black transatlantic resonance, one that was localised enough to feel familiar to West African listeners but equally global enough to feel familiar among the wider Black diaspora abroad. In some respects, it represents a continuum of community based Pan-Africanism without the heady political commentary Obrafour's debut LP is a rare standout with a body of work acclaimed for wise lyricism and reflection in the same way that Grime fanatics assess Dizzee's *Boy In Da Corner* or Hip Hop scholars refer to Nas's *Illmatic*. Very similar to Dizzee Rascal and Nas on their debut albums, Obrafour's *Pae Me Ka* is a commentary of the times from the important perspective of a young Black boy.

5

WXMEN IN AFROBEATS

Pioneering Ghanaian comedian Bob Johnson once said 'A girl on stage would be branded as a girl without morals.' Johnson's original quote was published in *The Story of Bob Johnson* in 1970 by Efua Sutherland (a revered playwright and activist who was also the first Black African woman to study at Cambridge). The statement remains an honest insight on attitudes toward women in popular entertainment in Africa and the diaspora today.

Highlife singers who were women in the early part of the 20th century were a rare phenomenon owing to traditionally patriarchal societies in West Africa. This attitude even filtered down to the very absence of women in concert parties both in the audience and on stage, leading to male singers struggling but attempting to sing the vocal tones that women would typically sing as stated in the excellent Ghanaian music blog Osibisaba. Therein lies the inherent juxtaposition the West African concert party form takes—as on the one hand it was a key factor in projecting new social attitudes to empower an impending new nation and cultural identity. Yet on the other it worked to push and promote patriachal ideals surrounding the role and position of women in West African society.

The concert party was a travelling art form that originated in the 1920s and was previously one of the major sources of entertainment that used to take part mostly in the villages of Ghana. Akin to a variety show in Britain, the concert party is a mixture of theatre, dance and music that portrays the multi-faceted African approach to art, with many of the plays often performed in local languages, audience participation and an educative aspect. It was based on the famous Ghanaian storytelling character of Ananse the spider which used to teach the public about morals blended with music. It eventually evolved inland becoming a popular tradition in cities across the country promoting cultural interaction among the diverse ethnic groups of Ghana in the 50s and 60s.

Despite highlife's relatively progressive roots when it came to providing messages that were previously only accesible for the upper echelon of Ghana, the genre continued to reinforce gender barriers that prevented women from being given a fair platform to express themselves. The expectation for women within West African society was to be a dutiful role wife and mother. Thus women choosing to have a career, least of all a music career, instead of having a family was an idea that was not accepted by society.

Concert parties and performances were a huge facet of the rise of highlife music with many shows performed during the night by live highlife bands. If a woman attended highlife shows alone or with friends, she would be deemed a prostitute , being asked the common question of 'where is your husband?'

The clash of new vs old in a newly independent nation like Ghana was a war of push and pull. On the one hand Ghana was a society with patriarchal ideas at its core, however, changes to the nation like independence and increased migration from rural villages to urban locations meant there was a gradual shift in mentality. This overall shift would result in a greater presence of women in West African music from the 1960s and onwards.

The influence of African-American singers associated with jazz and Swing Music in the 1930s via Ella Fitzegerald and Lena Horne would soon lead to African renditions of jazz songs. Renowned African music author and scholar John Collins recognised the impact firsthand and its gradual infiltration into the big band highlife scene post World War II. Julie Okine was one such example. Okine was the lead singer of E.T. Mensah's highlife band 'The Tempos'. She would become the first woman to join the group full-time. Her single 'Nothing But a Man's Slave' was considered by Collins to be 'the first feminist popular music song in Ghana.' Released in 1957 alongside a band heavily supported by the President elect Kwame Nkrumah, Okine was at the forefront of a movement that showed encouraging signs of a progressive new nation in Africa. The subsequent decade of the 1960s, which was post Ghana's independence in 1957, saw a number of newly independent African countries in their infancy. This new chapter in the continent provided space for a reimagination of cultural identity that would in turn result in state-led initiatives which facilitated wider contributions of women in mediums traditionally dominated by men.

Two major cultural examples where this shift occurred were at the Soul 2 Soul Festival in Ghana in 1971 and the Festac 77 festival in Nigeria in 1977. The former said to have been inspired by a James Brown gig in Lagos and suggested by the late African-American poet and activist Maya Angelou. It was produced by the American father and son duo Ed and Tom Mosk. Soul 2 Soul was held on 6th March 1971 and was scheduled from 3pm to 6am. The two day Independence celebration happened in Accra's Blackstar Square, and was a physical union where legendary African-American musicians appeared alongside Ghanaian acts. The first concert included heavyweight performances from Tina Turner, the Staple

Singers and Roberta Flack and the women members of the group Voices of East Harlem.

Interestingly, appearing on the same event lineup was also rising home-grown Ghanaian artist Charlotte Dada (also known as nee Daddah), where it is understood that she was the only Ghanaian woman artist on the bill. Dada was previously a vocalist from the Ghanaian highlife group 'The Uhuru Dance' Band and was dubbed as 'The Girl With the Golden Voice'. She is widely known for her 1971 cover of the Beatles song 'Don't Let Me Down'.

Dada's cover was released on the Decca West African Series label, a British music label that set up its first West African base in Ghana in 1947. Dada's version is grounded by the calm percussion of a cowbell and soft drums. Dada's voice flows atop the instruments and the singer finds space on her eulogy on the quest for everlasting love. She very much makes the song her own, making it dramatically distinguishable from the original 'Beatles' version. Dada was a pioneering enigma who like many talented polymaths was also a composer and actor, who according to Collins appeared in the 1972 film 'Doing Their Thing', the storyline of which involved a young girl who, against her father's wishes, becomes a soul singer.

The Decca West African Series label had a huge impact on Ghanaian recording artists. Set up in the capital of the country, Accra, the label would send sound engineers to Lagos to record consistently. This country to country travel was emblematic of how the cross-fertilisation of sounds could occur in West Africa.

Charlotte Dada was at the forefront of a label that soundtracked contemporary African music and would impact a new generation of young women who would find a rare role model in Dada.

A special shoutout must be extended to another Akan

recording artist called Janet Osei. In the early 70s Osei released her album 'Lovers Songs' in 1981, which featured songs she had written herself. Osei was also an actress, though she received more recognition for musicality.

Festac '77 in Nigeria would be a global diasporic celebration not seen at that time. The festival first occured in 1977 and is widely known as the second global Black and African Arts and Culture Festival. The festival would be an explosive gathering of Black musicians, activists, writers and creators from all over the world. Festac '77 occured alongside Nigeria's oil boom and the many riches that came with it. Festac '77 was a month long celebration of Pan-Africanism with delegates from over 60 countries including Australia and Brazil.

Among the one-hundred and fifty music and dance shows at Festac '77, one figure whose performance stood out was Miriam Makeba. Makeba was the first African musician to win a Grammy Award and the first African artist to headline a show at the Royal Albert Show (long before Wizkid in October 2017). Anchored in her traditional South African roots, Makeba brought African music to a global audience in the 1960s and stands as a benchmark for African women artists today .

Raised in pre-apartheid South Africa, Johannesburg, to be exact, the young Makeba would regularly sing as part of her school choir in her native language Xhosa* and English. At the age of 17, she joined the renowned Black Manhattan Brothers group, who rather like the previously mentioned concert party tradition in West Africa would provide South Africa with their own equivalent. The Black Manhattan Brothers were a South African musical group influenced by African-American musicality, taking inspiration from genres like jive and swing, as well native African genres. Makeba with the Black Manhattan

---

*   The most widely distributed African language in South Africa

Brothers would travel across neighbouring countries in Southern Africa. Her time with the group would come to an end once she got a lead role in the Broadway inspired musical *King King*, which was successful in her homeland and transferred to the West End in London during the early 60s. Each setting provided a fertile musical base for Makeba expanding her versatility.

Makeba's love of calypso and jazz music would put her on the radar of legendary musician and civil rights activist Harry Belafonte. Belafonte would help Makeba sign her first record deal in America. Harry Belafonte is an American musician who was born to a Jamacian mother and a Jewish father. He became synonymous with pop, calypso and crossing over folk into the US market. In the 1950s, when Makeba was making music in South Africa, the Apartheid government in heavily controlled the radio and recording industry. The government, enforced physical segregation through creating Black townships, this meant Black South African artists could not fully express their creativity out of fear of reprisal. Due to the heavily policed society, Makeba, like other South African artists of that era, was forced into unfortunate exile.

By the 1960s, the proverbial wall of separation between Makeba and her home, South Africa became increasingly politicised. At the same time, the Black Panther Party in the US was in full force and this impacted Makeba's relationship with music, seeing it as a safe space against Black oppression in America. Makeba would eventually decide to not sing in Afrikaans [the language predominantly spoken by the white apartheid government in South Africa] and fought to keep Xhosa alive in songs with titles like 'Qongqothwane'. Makeba's use of Xhosa was her attempt at keeping her heritage alive amidst the racist regime at home.

Makeba's shift from placid artist to forthright activist was very impactful at the time. Her anti apartheid perspective would soon see Makeba lose her South African citizenship and her music banned from her homeland.

Makeba once stated, 'in our struggle, songs are not simply entertainment for us. They are the way we communicate.'

A key recording by Makeba is the song 'Ndodemnyama we Verwoerd', which translates from Xhosa to 'watch out Verwoerd' and was released in 1965.

'Sophiatown is Gone' is another major recording from Makeba's discography that references a creative and influential location which fell under the apartheid government. The song was filled with clever lyricism that made the music appear elementary to the passive ear, yet music historian Anne Schumann notes, 'Sophiatown, near Johannesburg, was musically very active, the heart of the jazz and Mariabi scene at the time. It was also a thorn in the eye of the government, being a racially mixed area'. Subsequent laws in the Group Areas Act (1950) and the Prevention of Illegal Squatting Act (1951), soon initiated the removal of people from Sophiatown and a relocation to Meadowlands in Soweto. The deliberate degradation of a key epicentre for musicians is sung about in English with a cheerful tone, Makeba tops up what appears to be a positive punch until the goading banjo and drum halt for the last fourty seconds. What is left is Makeba's soaring acapella in the words, 'my folks are gone/the streets look sad and dry', a reflection of what exile had become for fellow South African jazz musicians like herself.

Released in 1977, 'Soweto Blues' was written by Hugh Masekela and sung by Makeba in response to the Soweto uprising of 1976—a series of demonstrations and protests led by Black schoolchildren in response to the introduction of Afrikaans as a compulsory language in secondary school education. The protests themselves saw over 10,000 Black students peacefully rallying together against the implementation of 'language of the oppressor' as Desmond Tutu called it. The masses were met by a hostile police presence and response whilst protesting on an alternative route after their initial planned route was barricaded. The police would soon react to the protesters by shooting directly at the children, killing up to over 700 unofficially estimated. This watershed event was a key moment in the anti-Apartheid movement. Makeba singing 'Soweto Blues' became a staple of her live performances in exile globally.

Makeba begins, 'the children got a letter from their master/ It said no more Xhosa, Sotho, no more Zulu.' This immediate reference reveals the struggle of the colonial mindset still alive despite being abolished officially. As the song resumes she croons in an ironic manner, 'that's when the policeman came to the rescue,' followed by a whistle. It signals a stand to attention and order, a piercing prequel to the pandemonium about to ensue. Makeba's spoken word and sung intonation style is deliberately done in the blues tradition, providing realism and commentary in dedication to the loss of a young generation.

Mandela once remarked, 'the curious beauty of African music is that it uplifts as it tells a sad tale… politics can strengthen music, but music has a potency that defies politics.' It's a reasoning and energy that would be attributed to Makeba as a person first and performer second.

Makeba's musical versatility in connecting Africa to the world via the Xhosa language and English led to the problematic term of 'World Music' being attached to her lengthy discography. Makeba's natural and early manifestation of cultural heritage alongside external influences was the precursor to women artists in Africa crossing over and using various genres. Her legacy was rooted in Black African pride and would go on to earn her the nickname 'Mama Africa'.

'Women are beginning to tell their men that they don't want to live a dull life… an empty one… women have been playing important roles in politics, hospitals and every aspect of life.' Truthful reflections from two women in Jeremy Marre's 1979 documentary *Konkombé: The Nigerian Pop Music Scene*, which followed the influential Lijadu Sisters in Nigeria in the 80s. Born Taiwo Lijadu and Kehinde Lijadu, the twins were second cousins of Fela Kuti. An inspirational and inseparable pair with the backing of a strong matriarch, born in the northern city of Jos in Nigeria, colloquially known as J-Town. Both of Yoruba descent, their tradition believes twins are magical and given protection by the Orisha Shango. Interestingly the Yoruba ethnic group mainly based in south-western Nigeria have the highest twinning rate in the world (4.4% of all maternities).

This highly favoured background informs the given names at birth in relation to who was born first and second. This fertile base emanating from a higher calling gave the Lijadu Sisters the power to be themselves and talk their truth without repercussions in an Afrobeat (without the 's') scene which had scarce female representation.

Their first EP *Iya Mi Jowo (Mother, Please)* came out in 1969 on the Decca West African Series Label. It had a B-side in Yoruba and a more widely known Swahili A-side titled 'Jikele-Maweni'. The Lijadu Sisters' magnetising harmonies swirl atop guiding and delicate guitar riffs with a talking drum gently grounding the music.

It's an inviting entry point into their discography with Nigeria on the ascent to an oil-rich boom which soon saw Decca relocate their main label headquarters from Accra to Lagos with a brand new recording studio in the heart of Nigeria. In the Konkombe documentary, the Lijadu Sisters reflect upon their reality in comparison to the influx of Western music labels, 'it's like you should be a baby to this company because you are actually making... money for them, but the other side of the coin is that they don't care.' This reflection in real time highlights their frustration with the industry at large and the lack of autonomy they had not only as African artists but as African women.

Influenced by Makeba the Lijadu sisters proudly inter-posed their love of jazz, Afrobeat and reggae in their music. Their musical style shattered attempts to pigeon-hole African artists. Much like their older cousin Fela Kuti, the Lijadu sisters took from different musical cultures whilst maintaining their strong sense of Africanness. Their brilliant musical fusion would eventually see the twins catch the attention of English drummer Ginger Baker. Baker was a huge Afrobeat fan who would join Fela's Africa '70 and soon set up his own Batakota (ARC) recording studio in Lagos, Nigeria. In 1973, Paul McCartney would travel with his band Wings to record at the studio. Baker and his studio highlight the early international appeal of the Afrobeat genre. Baker would become known as the Oyinbo (White) Drummer, and he would later invite the Lijadu sisters to perform with his band 'Salt' at the World Music Festival held in Munich, Germany, at the same time as the 1972 Olympics that summer. Around this time Kehinde and Taiwo would build a growing relationship with Nigerian multi-instrumentalist and producer Adeniyi 'Biddy' Wright. Wright's mother was a close friend of the sisters' mother, through whom the three met in the early 1970s. Wright co-arranged and played on all four of the classic 1970s Lijadu Sisters albums released on Decca's Afrodisia sublabel. Wright would assist in refining their Afro-funk style with the influx of new technology via synths and drum machines taking their music into the boogie and disco space. The sisters would sign to Afrodisia in the early 1970s and begin releasing the first of four LPs including *Danger*, *Mother Africa*, *Sunshine* and *Horizon Unlimited* from the mid-to-late 70s.

The first of their LPs released on Afrodisia was called *Danger* in 1976. A major single from the LP was called, 'Life's Gone Down Low', which is a mid-groove tempo funk-infused song. The song was a sonic reimagination for Nigerian youth post the civil war in the late 60s. The repeated loop of the song title is an honest assessment that references the internal effects of warfare on the mental health of those who experience it. However, the lyric of, 'a little bit of understanding/ but it's not too late for me and you if we hurry', hints at hope on the horizon and the possibility of reclaiming a new identity despite the impact of war. The song was a cathartic release which decades later would be sampled by African-American contemporaries in Nas, Madlib and Ghostface Killah.

I have a theory that third albums are often the mark of a new creative direction to swim into the mainstream after establishing a signature sound and loyal fanbase. However, with The Lijadu Sisters single 'Reincarnation' taken from their third LP *Sunshine* released in 1978, they were not reinventing themselves at all, in fact they were reaffirming their many musical influences ready for their loyal fanbase to devour. A delicate rocksteady reggae bass riff induces gentle head bops with stop-starts around the lines of, 'so be quick/take me there/bring me back home/where I belong.' The elongated stress on the word 'home' is akin to a wolf cry at the full moon and seems to perfectly capture their longing to return back. Perhaps due to the ancestral or mental state of being within the African diaspora, 'Reincarnation' was strong enough to appeal to the early generation of West African migrants across the globe.

The artwork of The Lijadu Sisters LP 'Sunshine' has the sisters sketched amidst nature in a desert plain. The imagery is shaded with pastel colours as the twins flank their raised arms to the beam of the low sun. The songs on this LP match the sentiment of the cover art, creating a care-free and empowering listening experience. In a rare interview with OkayPlayer in 2015, The Lijadu Sisters remarked on their approach to songwriting, 'when you make a song make sure people can pick that song and the tune 200 years later.' It is this process that has resulted in the longevity of their discography.

The Lijadu Sisters relocation to America in the 80s added to their sense of mystique. They visited the US with King Sunny Adé in 1988 and performed under their own name with Ade's band, and won an enthusiastic review in *The New York Times*. After the Ade concerts in the US, they stayed in the country while their green card applications went through. The pair's influence and activity didn't stop in the decades of their dominance, like all great artists they were able to reinvent themselves and maintain their cultural relevance. In 2014 they would go on tour with David Byrne from the band 'Talking Heads', Dev Hynes (also known as Blood Orange) and Kele Okereke (from the band 'Bloc Party') as part of the all-star 'Atomic! Bomb Band' to celebrate and pay homage to Nigerian electro-funk musician William Onyeabor. Taiwo and Kehinde Lijadu's hospitable personalities extended on the tour when they would provide a surprise spread of jollof rice, chicken and stew ahead of a live appearance on the *Tonight Show with Jimmy Fallon* in May 2014 for fellow performers. Sadly, Kehinde Lijadu suffered a stroke and passed in 2019 at the age of 71. Yet, the legacy of the Lijadu Sisters lives on through resonant reissues of their back catalogue.

Other notable mentions of women in West African music

in the late 70s to early 80s include Christy Essien-Igbokwe. Affectionately known as the 'First Lady of Song' in Nigerian pop music, her early LPs *Freedom* and *Patience* released under her pre-marital name Christiana Essien provides commentary on love, gender roles and African society in songs such as 'Mr. Boom Boom Boom,' 'Let's Face Our Problems' and 'I Don't Have To Cry (Cause You're Gone).' Often speaking and singing in a Country-Western style, the sombre percussive elements feel more like monologues. Essien-Igbokwe mixed rock and soul alongside the staples of disco and Afrobeat of that era.

On the sleeve notes of her third album *One Understanding*, released in 1979, the first of her subsequent releases on Decca's Afrodisia sub-label, Christy Essien-Igbokwe writes, 'when you have so much love and concern for the people of the world, the only way you can fight for them is by what you can offer.' It is a selfless mantra, which captures her approach in her life and music. Impressively, she was also a multilinguist who sang in her native language of Ibibio, a language native to southern Nigeria as well as in Igbo, Efik, Hausa, Yoruba and English. This gave her an instant platform to unite a Nigerian nation that was still recovering from their civil war just a decade earlier.

'Seun Rere', her most well-known single, would come from her sixth album *Ever Liked My Person?* released in 1981. Essien-Igbokwe was in her creative prime in this period, working with the influential producer Lemmy Jackson (a man likened to an African Quincy Jones) in Los Angeles. The majority of the tracklist on her LP have English song titles, a tell tell sign of her altering her direction in favour of crossing over to a more international market. Nevertheless, it would be the Yoruba sung 'Seun Rere' that became an intergenerational anthem continuing to unite Africans with her message. The message of the song was for children to heed the wise words of elders as well as highlighting the need for people to respect the young, who were still developing their view of the world.

At the time of the release of the LP *Ever Liked My Person?*, Essien-Igbokwe was only 21 years old. This would also be around the time that she would help establish the Performing Musician's Association of Nigeria (PMAN) with fellow renowned Nigerian artists King Sunny Ade and Sonny Okosun, where she would later become PMAN's first female president in 1996. She would use her status as a fearless personality to be a fervent supporter for the Performing and Mechanical Rights Society in Nigeria, regularly donating her own royalties to health and education programmes aiding women, children and the handicapped. An artist and humanitarian, Essien-Igbokwe's impact is unrivalled and was hugely influential for a generation of African artists who would come after her. She was a prime example of women artists using music as a vehicle for philanthropic movements, aligning themselves closer to the heritage of their parents.

In the early 1980s, Ghanaian gospel music from the local churches began to gain prominence. This coincided with the tough economic times Ghana was experiencing, Ghanaian gospel music was shielded from the economic turmoil as churches were viewed as charitable bodies and thus didn't have to pay entertainment taxes or the expensive import duty on musical instruments. As a result, many highlife musicians moved into gospel including Nana Kwame Ampadu and Francis Kenya. Women singers would dominate this music genre as many were happy to support women singing about God as opposed to worldy topics of highlife. It created an avenue for women recording stars, with local gospel repre-senting 60% of local music played on radio in 1990, and by

2002 over half of new gospel singers in the genre were women. Of the artists that were part of this development were another set of women twins called The Tagoe Sisters.

The Tagoe Sisters, individually known as Elizabeth and Lydia, have been a mainstay of the Ghanaian gospel scene for over three decades. The pair would initially find their voices whilst accompanying their late mother to the farm stating in an interview with the Ghanaian outlet Graphic Online, 'we improvis[ed] with empty milk tins as microphones to sing all day until it was time to return home.'

The Tagoe Sisters started singing in numerous ministries and churches as backing singers before releasing the soukous guitar-infused single 'Anka Matete' in 1997 alongside the album of the same name, which would go on to win the Best Gospel Album at the Ghana Music Awards that same year. The single 'Yedi Nkumim' is another classic from their popular discography, replete with synth brass keys, driving percussive drum backbeats and cosmic keys. The lyrics chorus roughly translates to, 'we are conquered, we are conquering and we will continue to conquer,' referring to battling adversity and using religion as a catalyst to survive. It is an uplifting song that provided inspiration to those of both a sacred or secular perspective.

For me, the song is the soundtrack of being in public transit with other passengers when going to visit my extended family members in Nkawkaw all the way to Kumasi in Ghana, both places where my parents originate from. At its core, the song is an oral guidance and introspective reflection of uncertainty when travelling long distances in Africa to meet the family.

Local Ghanaian churches and their new gospel highlife sound have become safe spaces for many parts of Ghanaian society including old-time highlife artists and women artists.

Just as the Black church in America provided a pathway

into the mainstream for women such as Mahalia Jackson and the later soul singers Aretha Franklin and Dionne Warwick. The Ghanaian church did the same for gospel singers like Esther Smith and Cindy Thompson who would cite the church and gospel music as a springboard that influenced their early experimentations within music and eventually the commercial Afrobeats scene.

With the rise of Afrobeats over the last decade, there has been a figure who has featured prominently in the wider music industry. She has been a backup singer to the likes of Chaka Khan and Mary J Blige and enrolled at the prestigious Berklee College of Music in Boston. This talented individual has also had a successful songwriting career writing for the likes of Babyface, Monica and Mya. However, her prominence in her own right would occur after relocating back to Nigeria from London in the early 2010s. Today, she is one of the most well known women of Afrobeats. This individual goes by the name of Tiwa Savage. Upon her return to Nigeria in 2012 Savage would sign with MAVIN Records. MAVIN Records was the freshly created label from Naija music head Don Jazzy in 2012 after the closure of his seminal music label Mo'Hits Records.

Don Jazzy's vision for MAVIN was for it to be the power house of African music.

The first time I would hear Tiwa Savage's voice was on the first release from MAVIN Records, a compilation album called *Solar Plexus*, released in 2012 and produced entirely by Don Jazzy. The album included an array of musicians, including Nigerian musicians D'Prince and Wande Coal.

Tiwa Savage's debut album *Once Upon A Time* was released in July 2013. In the aftermath of the album release, Savage stated in an interview with Nigerian newspaper *Vanguard*, 'this album is something that I really took my time with because I didn't want it to be the usual Nigerian album that contains party tracks from beginning till the end.' It is a telling remark that nods to her personal journey of leaving her homeland for the UK for a musical education. Savage's return back home was rooted in the desire to create a higher standard of music. It would be this attitude to create music with range and depth that would go on to cement her as an artist with impact and longevity.

'Kele Kele Love' was the lead single from Savage's debut album. It roughly translates from Yoruba as 'small small (love).' Savage floats between English and her mother tongue of Yoruba telling a lover to treat her and the relationship they have seriously, with a line of the chorus 'Ma Seri Beyen' affirming 'don't treat me like that'. The song was a singalong R&B banger which was successful and regularly played on radio stations like Choice FM and became a university rave favourite. Savage's mission to create the best possible music is best seen in her ability to collaborate with fellow musicians. On the hunt for interesting and boundary pushing sounds, Savage would work with music producers from the Black British and African-American parts of the African diaspora, a notable example of this is her work with London-born Nigerian producer Harmony Samuels. Samuels would produce two songs from Savage's debut including the lead single 'Kele Kele Love'. Through the lead single, the two would drive home a sound that brought together elements of electro and R&B that would appeal to both erudite Afro-pop enthusiasts and inquisitive European eardrums.

Other songs on her debut album portray a range of

emotion and international foresight that Savage had from early on in her career. 'Olorun Mi (My God)' was written in dedication to the lives lost in the Dana Plane crash in Nigeria in June 2012 where over 150 people died. The visuals for the song open with a dedication note to loved ones. Filled with figures dressed in white that appear to be spirits reincarnated from heaven with reflective shots of lost family members in a church setting. Savage redemptively calls 'O Lord my God' in the chorus. The song itself is a slow, country guitar riff mixed with a R&B ballad number. 'Olorun Mi' would be an early example of Tiwa Savage using her platform to give a voice to the voiceless in Nigeria—something that she would do more often as her career developed.

In the aforementioned interview with *Vanguard* in 2013, Savage was asked about her hopes for the Nigerian music industry to which she replied, 'I'd like us to be more international, be the pioneer of African music… I'd like a situation where I go to the UK and hear more [of] Nigerian music on radio and have our artists nominated for the Grammys.' Nearly a decade after this prophetic quote, Tiwa would leave MAVIN Records to sign her own deal with Motown Records. To date she has headlined her own concert at the indigo at London's The O2, become the first African woman ambassador for Pepsi and won the Best African Act at the 2018 MTV Europe Music Awards, becoming the first woman to win the category.

Tiwa Savage is a true consistent creative in the Afrobeats scene. As a bilingual African woman, Savage has surpassed many of her male counterparts despite the many attempts to discourage her path, she has even admitted that she considered quitting music but decided against it to show her son that she is not a woman who gives up. The Queen of Afrobeats continues to exude musical excellence, recently co-writing 'Keys To the

Kingdom' on the Beyoncé-led *The Lion King* soundtrack, *The Gift*.

Savage's sound is both gentle and strong. She has developed an impressive discography where her lyrics hypnotically move between English and Yoruba whilst singing about patriarchy, love, money and societal issues. As Savage gets deeper into her impressive career, her voice has only gotten louder and not just in music. We have seen her use her platform openly, speaking about her attempts to bleach her skin, expanding on the pressures of Black women in the music industry but more specifically darker-skinned African women.

Tiwa has addressed the issue of rape and sexual assualt in Nigeria, which she asserts is a massive issue in her home country. Savage has gone as far as providing legal aid to victims of rape in Nigeria. Savage once took to her Instagram story with the statement, 'it is a sin to be a woman in Africa. I feel like giving up; I am tired of fighting; I am tired of proving myself; I am tired of smiling.' A strong and moving statement that speaks to the core of much of Savage's activism and also the struggle of women within Africa. Savage was one of the many Nigerian artists who used their platform to speak about the #EndSARS movement that exploded in 2020.

For Savage humanity is more important to her than music as she stated in an interview with *The Guardian* in 2020. Much like the women who came before her, many of whom have been mentioned in this chapter, Savage's spirit embodies the strength of women in African music and Afrobeats. After decades in the industry, Savage has become an inspiration for Nigerian women and African women alike.

Within the hiplife era of the 2000s, a number of female artists released music concurrent to the men of the genre. As I discussed in the 'hiplife' chapter, we have Mzbel, whose single '16 Years' commented on misogyny and sexual abuse within Ghana. The song is sung in Pidgin English and Akan. The choral refrain asserts Mzbel's unapologetic attitude for expressing her dress sense and body image as she wants. The visuals of the song are centred around an open court room where an 'uncle' is in the dock facing trial for his sexual abuse and harassment of the lead character played by Mzbel. The music video ends with the judge finding him guilty and sentencing him to prison. Here we see a link between Tiwa Savage's activism for victims of rape in Nigeria with Mzbel's depiction of a tragically similar reality in the sexual assualt in Ghanaian society.

Mzbel would inspire a new generation of women artists in Ghana including Tiffany, Sister Deborah and the late Ebony. Reigns Ghanaian musician Ebony Reigns was born Priscilla Opoku-Kwarteng in 1997. She would become known for her signature style of fluidly moving between rapping and singing in an Afro-pop- and dancehall-influenced style. Ebony released her single 'Sponsor' in 2017. Ebony shows clarity and confidence in the accompanying visuals where she openly chronicles the merits of a 'sugar daddy' financially and sexually. An older man (played by her real dad) is seen throughout the video treating and looking after Ebony with cutaway shots featuring her amongst her girl crew dancing.

In 'Sponsor', Ebony speaks on the difference between a broke boyfriend and a wealthy gentleman. She honestly addresses things like her vagina hurting from sexual intercourse and sexually pleasing herself despite the number of suitors she has access to. The video ends with Ebony subverting typical gender norms as she makes a 'booty call'.

The song would go on to win Afro-Pop Song of the Year at the Vodafone Ghana Music Awards in 2018, that same night would also see her album *Bonyfied* which included 'Sponsor' collect the Album of the Year. Ebony Reigns would top the award ceremony off by winning the Artist of the Year award becoming the first woman to do so.

Ebony's musical style was understood to be a fusion of dancehall and Afrobeats; her rapid success led to her becoming one of Ghana's most popular rising Afrobeats acts. She owned her sexuality and refused to alter her expression even when she faced public criticism within her country. She would release songs like 'Maame Hw3' that would explore issues of domestic violence and 'Aseda', which looked at the challenges of being a woman in the entertainment industry. Ebony in many ways was the musical daughter of Mzbel, particularly in her spirit and boldness. Both women refused to bend to the will of the patriarchal societies from which they came and made a deliberate effort to challenge the views of women within Ghana and consequently Africa. Tragically Ebony would pass away in February 2018, just a week before her 21st birthday. The cause of her death was a car crash in Accra after visiting her mother.

Ebony Reigns was only musically active for two years before her death, and her passing was seen by many as a huge loss for African music. Within Ghanaian society, Ebony Reigns was viewed as a controversial figure. Her art divided listeners; many found her empowering and brave whilst others believed her music to be sinful. In a traditional and patriarchal society like Ghana, her sexual assertiveness and expression caused societal friction and unease to say the least. Ebony's confidence and legacy shifted conversations in Ghana far more rapidly than many of her predecessors.

Other notable mentions in the trajectory rise of women in Afrobeats include the new age 'Mama Africa' in Nigerian Afro-pop singer Yemi Alade. A multilinguist hailing from Abia

State, Nigeria; Alade speaks seven languages including French, Yoruba, and Swahili. Her versatility in using different African languages in her songs has cemented her global appeal. Her most catchy and well known hit 'Johnny' released in 2014 and was an international hit. At the time of writing this book the music video to 'Johnny' holds the YouTube record for the most watched African Female music video of all time. Alade has since collaborated with Beyoncé on 'Don't Jealous Me', a song taken from *The Lion King: The Gift* film soundtrack and showed her creativity as an actress featuring in its visual companion *Black Is King*.

Alade looks to be one of Afrobeats most promising female artists. In 2020, Yemi Alade became a Goodwill ambassador for the United Nations Development Programme. Alade said she would use her position to focus on empowering women, combatting inequality as well as raising awareness about climate change.

In 2013, an Afrobeats artist was nominated for the Most Promising Female Act to Watch at the Nigeria Entertainment Awards. Her name was Lola Rae. Rae is a Nigerian born singer and dancer of Ghanaian and British heritage who rose to prominence from British talent show Britain's Got Talent in 2010. After success on the show and signing to Simon Cowell's Syco label, Rae would return to her academic studies and later had the blessing of her parent's to pursue music full-time. In 2012 Lola Rae would release perhaps her biggest song to date 'Watch My Ting Go' in 2012 produced by P2J . The song was inspired by Rae's time working in a club in London and celebrated the different shapes and sizes of young African women, and the way they moved. The song would be a popular song in the UK university rave scene. In more recent times, she has released singles with the likes of Davido, who featured on 'Biko' in 2016, the single 'Shower Me,' produced by Juls and released in 2020, and the smooth jam 'Come and See' in April 2021.

In mid-December 2019, I sheltered myself from the midday heat in Accra's fashionable East Legon as I waited in a trendy café. A mixture of international school alumni and expats sipped their freshly blended smoothies whilst staring aimlessly into MacBooks with blank Word documents open. The loop of crushing coffee beans threatened to overwhelm my planned interview with a peroxide-haired figure who sauntered over to me in an incognito manner. There, my interviewee was in stylish sunglasses and an impeccably trendy denim outfit. Noticing the star's presence, a few customers turned their necks in an ostrich-like fashion, yet Amaarae seemed completely oblivious to the attention.

Warm and apologetic for the late arrival owing to the hazardous Ghanaian traffic, Amaarae eventually sits opposite me and we begin our talk. Her initial reclusive presence online has opened up on her records, 'Fluid' and 'Like It' where an assured image confronting androgyny and sexuality belie a non-conformist personal expression. Her music is a steadfast tribute to individuality and being proud of showing the multiple identities an African can inhabit.

Born Ama Serwah Genfi, Amaarae is a singer, producer, songwriter and sound engineer. She was born in the Bronx, New York, in 1994 and raised between Ghana and the United States. Despite the physical movement, Amaarae's African identity was drummed into her by her mother. She reminisces, 'I have an African mum and she never let me forget that. Not only does she speak local dialect like Twi to us, but our customs and traditions didn't change because we were living in America.'

A fan of British-born singer Corinne Bailey Rae (an inspiration for Amaarae's own stage name), Amaarae also cites hiplife artists as influential role models growing up, namechecking Ofori Amponsah and Obrafour. However, it is the mention of a particular hiplife artist that leaves Amaarae visibly excited. The artist's name is none other than Daasbre Gyamenah. On Gyamenah, Amaarae says, 'Daasbre Gyaminah's [song] 'Kokokoko', it actually takes the drums and bassline of Brandy's 'U Don't Know Me (Like U Used To).' That tune is a mad mad tune.'

It's an adage she applies in her own right as a producer. 'I always start with a melody and then the lyrics fall into place after,' she says. She further notes how her lyricism comes through subconsciously, 'I think for me a lot of the things I say will have something to do (with something) that happened a week before.' I query her on the emergence of solidarity between Ghanaian and Nigerian artists in the alté scene a la the highlife and Afrobeat band age in the 60s and 70s. She notes the safe space with the neighbours east of Ghana. 'I'd say that the alté scene in Nigeria welcomed me first and the first person I collaborated with was an artist called AYLØ… from me working with him… I built those relationships that way.'

Amaarae's Soundcloud bio previously read, 'Pro shawty wiv da bald head,' her music is euphoric and imaginative as her visuals. She is proud to bring Ghana to the world and inspire experimentations well out of any comfort zone. Witnessing her mesmeric stage presence firsthand during a cameo appearance with Major Lazer dancing in the refurbished Sandbox club venue in Accra in 2019 with a passionate fan, Amaarae is one to watch in the booth and on the boards. Amaarae is testament to how the music scene in Ghana and Nigeria has developed. With the acclaimed release of her debut album *The Angel You Don't Know* in November 2020 filled with Afro-pop fusions across alté, R&B, Southern rap, dancehall and punk rock references. She is part of the new school of women who seek to maintain their heritage and push music culture, redefining what it means to be young, Black and African in the diaspora.

Amaarae's single *Sad Girlz Luv Money* from her album *The Angel You Don't Know* would go on to receive chart success in 2021. Amaarae described the song as 'an anthem, an affirmation, a prayer, a movement' in *Crack Magazine* in February 2021. The same year, Kali Uchis would jump on the remix and the single would chart at 80 on the US Billboard Hot 100.

At the time of writing this book, another young woman exploded onto the Afrobeats stage. Known for her velvety, addictive vocals, Temilade Openiyi was born in Lagos in June 1995. This Nigerian songstress has already been dubbed the future of this growing genre. Better known as Tems, the young star has already worked with global superstars, attained two US top 40 songs on the Billboard Hot 100,and found fans in stars like Rihanna and Adele.

2020 was a big year for Tems. Her sultry vocals on the global hit *Essence* by Wizkid would catapult her to stardom leading everyone wanting to know who the star in the making was. Today, Tems is very much the princess of Afrobeats, who is as talented, as she is enigmatic. The song *Essence*, whilst Wizkid's song, was very much cemented by Tems's presence on the track, which Justin Bieber called 'the song of the summer'. In 2021, Bieber jumped on the remix, which would earn Tems a Grammy nomination. and was generally considered a marker moment in the internationality of Afrobeats. Tems has since collaborated with international superstar Drake on the song *Fountains* on his 2021 album *Certified Lover Boy*. In Semptember of that year, Tems released her second EP *If Orange Was A Place*. The EP garnered great reviews and reached the top ten Billboard World Albums chart.

The presence of women in Afrobeats brings a sauce that continues to elevate the genre (both in front of the camera and behind the scenes). The reality of being a woman artist on the African continent and in the diaspora is challenging, yet they continue to persevere. They constantly push their creativity further, often experimenting with different styles and sounds. The alté scene in particular is a musical alternative where gender fluidity challenges the patriachal stranglehold of Afrobeats. Women artists in Africa have been important catalysts in the progression of this fast developing genre. Proving time and time again that they often think outside of the box and intentionally challenge societal expectations and Western preconceptions, elevating African music in the 21st century.

6

THE SKANKING ERA—
UK FUNKY HOUSE

The year is 2007, it is autumn. My A-Levels are finally over and I am about to embark on the next part of my academic journey—it is time for university! Growing up in London meant I had a unique relationship with the nightlife of the city. Like many who have resided in a metropolitan city, when it came to partying I was spoilt for choice. However, being spoilt for choice did not mean I always had a smooth experience. Some of my most treasured memories would include trips to a West End club called Moonlighting, before ending up in Soho and finally finding myself trickling down the N29 bus route (RIP the free bendy party bus).

Friday nights were the centre of London's vibrant clubbing scene, equipped with nights like 'Club NME' or 'Buttoned Down Disco' at KOKO (a concert venue in the heart of Camden). These nights would give attendees the sweet sounds of a trendy band or a solo newcomer often performing indie, disco or electro music. These were the nights where I would find home-grown and DIY artists to follow on MySpace (my fresh-faced profile is still lurking somewhere… search if you must).

This was a time where I was seeking my path to

independence. The safety blanket of EMA* had been removed thus I had to be mindful of how my limited finances were to be used. Money for London transport does not grow on trees - so I had to make a decision. For me this meant avoiding Ghanaian hall parties in favour of attending nights I deemed to be cool enough

After those early summers of return to Ghana as a child, I was now entering young adulthood, and my connection to the motherland became increasingly distant.

I had originally intended to study in Aberdeen, Scotland, to get as far away from London not only in a physical sense, but mentally too. I soon came to the realisation that the only way I could take all my belongings that far north would be to shout Abracadabra. Eventually, I would opt for somewhere a little closer to London. This place was called Canterbury and was where I would attend the University of Kent for the next three years.

My first week on campus was a whirlwind. I remember taking in the green settings and having to adapt very quickly to sharing basement-style accomodation and reluctantly drinking snakebite pints (a cheap alcoholic drink from the UK). Amidst the heavy nightlife schedule during Freshers Week, I wanted to get a headstart with the Reading list for my course (very responsible, right?). So I made my way to the imposing campus library called The Templeman. As I walked up the tired carpet stairs, I scanned my card in and began to search for the relevant books, desperate to cure my hangover with a hardback. It wasn't long before I heard a faint whisper of, 'hi, excuse me' behind me. I turned and there was a welcoming smile and a badge with the letters 'ACS'. There she was, a young Black

_____

*   Education Maintenance Allowance is a financial scheme applicable to students and those undertaking unpaid work-based learning in the United Kingdom. It was previously available in England until it ended in October 2010.

girl around my age with a London accent talking in relentless speed akin to a jungle MC. Possibly noticing my slight confusion she slowed down her words and softly repeated, 'would you like to sign up to the ACS?'

The last three letters were as foreign to me as a slice of quiche is to an eskimo. What on earth was an ACS? I soon would learn that this was an acronym for 'African Caribbean Society' and unbeknownst to me at the time, the ACS would gradually reignite a new sense of pride in celebrating my heritage and the heritage of fellow Black people in my university.

My ACS journey would be rooted in music, particularly UK funky house and its intersection with the university rave scene.

As an 18-year-old Black kid from North London, Black British music influenced me heavily. I can remember an 'urban music' talent show in my school where the youngers rapped '21 Seconds' by So Solid Crew, and other classics that the mandem felt spoke to them. Just as music formed the centre of our young idenitity, so did fashion with a plethora of mandem rocking Air Max, Akademiks tracksuits and New Era caps (with the sticker left on). During this time, many of us dreamt of becoming the next Dizzee Rascal or Skepta. This was and still is part of who I am.

So now, here I am, at the start of my university journey and the breadth of UK funky house music welcomes me in. UK funky house was a change, bereft of the overt masculine relief and heavy bravado that the genres like Grime and Garage held. More than anything it was an invitation to dance and sweat. UK funky was about following the carefree flavour felt in borrowing the sounds felt in Trini soca chimes, bashment's self-assured bass and the polyrhythmic jams of highlife and Afrobeat—to me, it was musical bliss. Providing succinct definitions of musical styles and genres is never easy because they never do it justice and UK funky house is no different. If you are not familiar with the genre, I urge you to go forth and bless your ears, but if one had to attempt to define UK funky house, I would say it is a genre that fuses tribal, soulful house sounds with Afrobeat, grime electro, break beat and garage, uniting the Black Atlantic on the dance floor.

UK funky is a sonic identity created in the United Kingdom as an audio sum of experiences felt through the children of West African and Caribbean parents. When we speak about UK funky house , there is one individual who has been synonymous with the genre since its emergence. His spacey blipped banger of a song called 'My Philosophy (Bounce)' was released in 2003. He also had his own early UK garage crew *Bubbling* in the late 1990s and would go on to collaborate with most of the UK's most prominent Black British acts. Ian Greenidge better known as Donae'O is the legendary singer-songwriter and producer from Norf Weezy (North-West London to the uninitiated). Donae'O is an effortlessly successful cross-genre chameleon. The breadth of his discography is truly impressive and in many ways represents the variety of sounds within the Black British community. His career encompasses so many sounds from UK garage, grime alongside bassline and dubstep, Afrobeats, and as of late he has crisscrossed sonically as seen in his productions for Giggs in Lock Doh' and Linguo.

Yet it is his UK funky discography filled with call and response catalysts in 'Party Hard', 'Devil in a Blue Dress' and 'African Warrior' from his *Party Hard* album in the summer of 2009 which held particular resonance for Black British youngsters at the time. The album acknowledges the shared sense of dual identity that many Black British people have whether that be those whose parents originate from the Caribbean or Africa. Donae'O himself is a product of Ghanaian and Guyanese parents and thus the diversity of Blackness is something he knows all too well.

'African Warrior' from the *Party Hard* album is a single that has found staying power over a decade after its release. It was an obvious reference point for those of African descent and their allies (alie) to proudly skank,on the dance floor. In the song Donae'O proudly asserts, 'I'm an African warrior.' Now, perhaps today this doesn't seem particularly profound, but one must remember that this song was released before the Afrobeats wave and before African identity was celebrated in the mainstream. Thus, Donae'O's proud assertion held major significance as it allowed those of African descent to feel pride when the song came on. Interestingly, the hit started off as a joke, but upon further reflection Donae'O realised how important and empowering this song could be.

Africanness among the Black British community was viewed very differently in the 90s to early 2000s. It was not considered cool or desirable. There were also cultural tensions between Caribbeans and Africans, where it was generally seen that to be Caribbean was more desirable than to be African.

On a podcast appearance with award-winning comedian Mo Gilligan in 2020, Donae'O further reflected on the impact of African Warrior as a pacifying peace anthem amidst the diaspora wars, he said, 'people are coming up to me saying you've destroyed the divide between Africans and West Indians now. I didn't realise how Africans really felt. [They're telling me] we're in a rave and the only time we hear our songs is when we go to house parties. When 'African Warrior' came on they all ran on stage and had something to sing but then the West Indians were singing it as well.'

The unmistakable onomatopoeic siren cry of 'Doh-Nay-Oh' would precede DJ sets as me and my peers were dressed in our Arab Shemagh scarfs, polo shirts and Primarni (also known as Primark) plimsolls. Donae'O's music and UK funky as a whole was a lively catalyst transforming raves into soggy sweatboxes of bedlam, strong B.O. and trips to the smoking area to get "some fresh air" .

Being of Guyanese and Ghanaian heritage, Donae'O's unique ability in crafting music came from his own lived experience. In an interview I conducted with him in 2011 for a *Guardian* article, he said, 'in Africa, they're not looking to make a catchy tune and you can see that as they consistently make hits… I think African artists and musicians… make better music.' His epiphany came after time spent living in Ghana. Donae'O in many ways represents the connection of UK funky to early Afrobeats, the timing of which coincided with an impressionable young Black student population entering higher education in the UK and partying to the sounds of UK funky. 'I grew up listening to drum and bass, garage and I naturally gravitated to African-style beats. I started to research and find African house like kwaito and azonto,' Donae'O said. 'I was influenced by African music and I started making funky… it was already in my blood.'

In the same phone interview, I recall him being excited and very aware of the various strands of house music on the continent that were united by the polyrhythms noting the spread of his own tune 'Party Hard', which sampled soulful house track 'We Belong To The Night' by Canadian producer Suges.

'It's not like I meant this to happen or I gave them to any Ghana, Nigerian or American DJs and we blew up. I put out 'Party Hard' myself, promoted it and [it] took a life of its own.'

The last 20 years in the UK has seen music serve as an cultural reference for children of West African heritage particularly those from Ghana and Nigeria. It has become something that reinforces a sense of community and pride. Through cultural events such as independence day events, the recent development of festivals celebrating African music and the rapid rise of music from the continent holding space in media, popular culture, books (hey!) and TV. The development and staying power of modern Africanness in music has cemented itself in not just Black Britishness but international Blackness.

In Martha J. Chinouya and Peter J. Aspinall's book *The African Diaspora Population In Britain*, this shift in population domain is reinforced as the authors state that, 'The Black African population in England & Wales stood at almost 1 million larger than Black Caribbean and other Black groups combined.' The pair found that in the 2011 England & Wales Census, 'on the measure of people with degree-level qualifications, Black Africans had the third highest percentage (40%) after the Chinese (43%) and Indians (42%).' The rise in this Black African population and their route into higher education would soon plant the seeds for the influential rave scene and early wave of UK Afrobeats that would emerge from the Afro-Caribbean societies of key universities around the M25 including Brunel, Hertfordshire, and Kingston university, and in the East Midlands with Nottingham Trent, De Montfort, Coventry university and many more. This provided an opportunity for young resourceful event promoters and ravers to connect with a slightly more mature version of youth clubs that some attended in the 'ends'.

'I was putting my name next to flyers so it was easier to get venues. So them lot (Mista Silva etc) started jumping on funky as MCs and it was the rise of funky house artists that we worked with.' Reflecting on the initial discrimination toward Black run events and adopting his own alias, Mikeal Silva aka Philip Owusu was a promoter in the early 2000s university rave era.

Mikeal noticed a gap in the events space for young students of African heritage across the UK. He would steadily build an in-house network of entertainers, promoting their musicality under the Silva name. Along with his business partner Will Oherien, President of the Afro-Caribbean Society (ACS) at De Montfort University, Owusu began a journey into curating events for the Black student population in the East Midlands, many of whom were originally from London .

'We were all out there and all wanted to enjoy parties that symbolised us and identified our cultures and stuff'. This attitude would sow the seeds for Mikeal's early foray into the student events scene. Mikeal continues, 'in 2003/4, we looked at Leicester, De Montfort, Birmingham University and realised there is actually a market for this. So we called it CoachParty. Com and built a website. (We put it on) every three months during term time and we grew (our audience) from 400 to 2,000 people in two years.'

As the Midlands market started to become more saturated, Mikeal's focus would move back toward London and South-East England in the late 2000s, collaborating with upcoming promoters on events such as the popular yet short lived 'I Luv Uni' at Sound in Leicester Square. Eventually Mikeal and his team would create their own nightclub brands for events including Silver Bunnies, Silver Mistletoes and If You're On This Let Me Know and others. During this time Mikeal sensed another avenue for event promotion through a mix CD. This was the pre-smartphone and music streaming era where poor quality YouTube videos were converted into MP3's for music players and Mikeal's simple yet smart idea of a mix CD filled another gap in the university rave market. The mix CDs would be hosted by MCs and allow ravers to revise the songs that would be played at the event they would be attending. It gave party-goers the chance to party before the party and immerse themselves in sing-a-longs and skanks.

Mikeal reflects, 'we started to notice that we had an influence as we had a captive audience and we realised that if we could influence music and put a few of our own artists on a few songs either singing or that they were involved in, we can get their songs listened to.' He adds, 'when people had a CD they were happy and that CD could be stuck in someone's car for two months. So we started printing 2 to 3,000 CD's every rave.'

Using the fast-growing UK funky scene as a vehicle for their raves, upcoming artists were having success across the UK. The genre's growing popularity would soon see it cross-over into the mainstream and inadvertently saturate the scene with younger promoters down South. The transition from UK funky to Afrobeats would shift events from local universities to wide ranging events in Europe.

In the early 2010s, Mista Silva would make the first steps from university rave MC to artist leading the early wave of a diasporan sound after a trip to Ghana. 'Even though he is British-born he was very much in touch with his Ghanaian roots,' Mikeal says on our intermittent video call and continues, 'one day he came back and started noticing that other artists from Africa were doing well. So you had all these artists that were starting to blow you had WizKid, E.L and the beginning of the skanking songs, which was very similar to funky house. You had a similar sound with 'Azonto' (Fuse ODG) so Mista Silva did a track with Kwamz, Flava and A-Star called 'Bo Wo Sem Ma Me'. So we put that song on a CD and it did very, very well.'

This versatile MC who emerged from Grime roots in his teens would find a sense of home in UK funky house and Afrobeats. Born as Papa Kwame Amponsa hailing from Ghana via South-East London, Mista Silva was the first unsigned UK Afrobeats artist to have his music playlisted by UK Radio Station BBC 1XTRA.

I first watched Mista Silva emerge onto the university rave scene in the latter part of 2009 as part of the 'Fresh 2 Def Collective' who ran music events for ACS's at universities across the UK.

Silva reflects on his early connection to West Africa and the turning point which resulted in his emergence: 'I would go out with my friends to Ghana Independence [a event celebrating Ghanaian Independence day]. I would know about African genres but it wasn't a cool thing [like it is now]. When I went to Ghana, I got more in tune with the African side of myself.' Silva added, 'I respected where I came from even more because I am in the root of it all and I took time to think about it.' Spending time in a place that is not quick to commodify your experience saw Mista Silva return back to the UK with clarity. It would be the sounds of UK funky that provided a reflective Mista Silva the outlet to pursue musical experimentations that spoke to his dual identity. He says, 'I came back and the sound which was popping was UK funky but that funky house sound had a very African tribal-orientated sound behind it and it led me to orientate my lyrics in a more African way.'

During his time as a university rave MC, Mista Silva's cadence blended within Twi and English. This was an effortless masterclass in code switching, finding space between himself and the DJ whilst maintaining the ravers attention. I recall his impactful ad-libs of 'Eh Papa' and 'Kah-de-boom ah go down low' that for me, evoked personal memories of being at family events. Mista Silva reflects upon his initial impact within the university rave scene: 'People were just like "Rah! This guy is just doing what he feels." He doesn't have no fear and people are responding to it. It felt like some mad power. Whether you were African, Caribbean or whatever country you come from you're going in with it. That alone was crazy.'

As a young Black man growing up in London, being caught 'slippin' (being in an area you're not supposed to be in) was a point of concern, but this African-infused music created a new sense of solidarity amongst the Black British community. Just as it was normal to rep one's area, now it was becoming normal to rep your parents' heritage. Mista Silva's lexicon much like Donae'O's music provided a ceasefire to plantain pronunciation wars. Mista Silva would bring young adults of African heritage and Caribbean heritage to the dance floor, magically evaporating cultural tensions that existed within these two Black British identities.

The opportunity to tease Twi over UK funky gave Mista Silva the confidence to come into his own even more. He saw an opportunity to make sense of his new-found self and attracted those with a similar upbringing. 'People were like why don't you do an Afrobeats track. I don't think anyone was brave enough and even I thought initially it wouldn't work.' He speaks further, 'I eventually ended up doing it with Kwamz, Flava and A-Star (fellow UK Afrobeats allies of Ghanaian heritage). We just started linking up spitting over beats and instrumentals then we had Ghana Party In The Park (one of the UK's biggest annual events celebrating Ghanaian culture). We thought why not make a Ghana Party In The Park anthem.' That anthem would soon become 'Bo Wo Sem Ma Me' (clap your hands for me). The track borrows a Ghanaian instrumental from group 5ive 5ive's popular track 'Move Back (Muje Baya)', a popular early azonto anthem released in 2011. They rode on the song's initial popularity through dance videos, spreading the sound uniting Africa and the UK.

Produced by prominent Ghanaian music producer Appietus, the instrumental has a constant piano loop which serves as the baton-led refrain that induces your feet to move instantly.

The video itself speaks to our community through its centered location of the barbershop. The barbershop in the Black community is a sacred place, one where lost and found hairlines are cared for by seasoned and talented hair surgeons (also known as barbers). I cannot begin to explain the level of trust one must have to let someone take care of the most prized part of a personal portfolio the way that men do with their barbers. In the video for 'Bo Wo Sem Ma Me', the barber shop serves as an open listening party for the track. Mista Silva reflects on the impact of the song, 'I was popular in funky house but I wasn't blowing innit. Whereas when I jumped on that Afrobeat ting it gave man an insight and opened my eyes like yo chale. You have to follow this as this is your culture and look how it's pushing you more.'

Silva also notes the support of his Fresh 2 Def collective who regularly ran those UK funky nights at the height of the university rave era in the early 2010s where they would include a number of hall party classics in their DJ sets. 'I felt like there are other Africans from across the country that go to uni in Manchester, Birmingham and Leicester… you name it. You go there, you give out your CD's and when they come back to London (or wherever) They say "I was listening to Silva…" saying, "that guy that was sick."' He further says, 'It was our leadership, we pushed it throughout universities to establish where we are now today.'

As an early figure who spoke to the transitions of Black subcultures from London to the wider African diaspora, Mista Silva reminds me that Silva is actually an acronym which stands for Strong Inspirational Live (And) Versatile Artist.

Another figure who rose from the mid-2000s UK funky 'uni rave' era is label owner P Montana. P Montana is synonymous with UK funky's transition to this current wave of Afro sounds,

A student of Ghanaian descent hailing from Grime's original epicentre of East London, P Montana was introduced to DJing by DJ Funkz, he was among the first to push subgenres like Afro-bashment and Afro-swing. Now head honcho of independent label Rah Boy Records, a title taken from a cult ad-lib used to herald early mixes blending hip hop, highlife and latterly Afrobeats. P Montana is a figure who personifies the grassroots development of the first wave of African-influenced music in the UK this past decade.

On a typical British day in early Spring 2019, I met P Montana at Rah Boy HQ near Woolwich in South-East London. It is an area which still has innumerable military and naval monuments that hint at its previous guise as the chief dockyard of the British navy. Its close proximity to the southern bank of the River Thames also made it a key industrial town for a little thing called the British Empire. During our discussion, I prompt him to reflect on what sparked his initial interest in the early days of African music. 'When you did listen to Afrobeats, it was always throwbacks. So you would hear stuff like Daddy Lumba, Ofori Amponsah, Mzbel.' It would be this musical exposure of highlife and hiplife that would impact his later musical achievements.

P Montana speaks more on this: 'You start going to university raves (around 2010)… [then]hiplife and Afrobeats starts to kick off properly in this [second] generation because I was old enough to remember how it sounded back then but was old enough now to go out and enjoy it properly.' P Montana's experience, captured the start of African sonics entering the Black British cultural circuit. It was a time that expanded the British multicultural monolith and widened what it meant to be Black in Britain.

P Montana continues, 'you had DJs like myself, Neptizzle and Afro B playing a lot of old school Afrobeats in the clubs.' He also notes the influence of an emerging wave of UK artists experimenting with the Afrobeats sound in the UK. 'You had artists like Mista Silva, Kwamz and Flava also breaking through the underground; this was just after 2010. So that was when the first phase of Afrobeats kicked off in London.' Today, it is easy to say that Afrobeats looked like a trend that globalisation would sweep up; but, at the time the scene was flourishing predominantly under the radar, in its own paradigm far from anything mainstream. P Montana agrees with my point and further adds, 'a song that came out yesterday would be the biggest song in the club in the uni scene… A lot of the things happening underground didn't translate into statistics or mad numbers in sales, but there was a demand for it which you couldn't put on paper.'

THE DJ AND THE MIX CD

As mentioned, mix CD's played a huge role in the emergence of UK funky house and Afrobeats around this time. The mix CD was usually curated by DJs, often handmade, recorded and burned for an eager partying audience. It was a true D.I.Y. endeavour and would give emerging DJs the chance to secure future bookings and gain a new audience. These mix CD's would serve as a welcomed teaser until the next funky rave. When we speak of the development of the UK funky and eventually Afrobeats scene, it must be remembered just how pivotal DJs were in its development.

One rising selector who emerged as a student in the UK was DJ Larizzle. Hospitable, informative, and award-winning, the now-record-label-owner has been one of the leading tastemakers in Afrobeats and Afro-house over the last decade.

DJ Larizzle helped introduce the sounds of Afrobeats to the Ayia Napa* club scene in the late 2000s. His enrollment at the University of Surrey in the mid 2000s would lead to a pivotal encounter with DJs at his student union who played at nights held by the university's African Caribbean Society (ACS). He explains this to me whilst we are sitting in a warm members club in the autumnal chill of Central London in 2019. A juxtaposition to the light, sunkissed sounds which Larizzle has become known for blending. 'I thought DJing was a good way of allowing me [to play multiple genres]. I liked so many genres of music I thought this was the best way of incorporating all of that in terms of performing.'

I ask about the attraction of the ACS during university. He responds, 'they (ACS) really represented Africa. Diaspora. Especially in Guildford (Surrey), which was a predominantly white university. I was drawn to the ACS because of the like minded people… from my background who attended and we all came together to do events.' Larizzle recalls his secondary school days as the foundation for the DJ mixes he would create during university, 'the energy was free. It took me back to my sixth form… I would be the one to compile compilations of music and distribute it amongst my friends. My nickname was Lazza… I called it Lazzamix 1.' Larizzle, like many emerging DJs of that time, relied on resourceful creativity to push themselves forward in an emerging culture. He delves into this when explaining how he distributed his mix CD in Ayia Napa during the formative years of UK funky in the late 2000s. 'I called the mix series *Strictly Funky* and I would duplicate it onto CD. When I used to go to Ayia Napa (a lot), I would take loads with me, hundreds and fill my suitcase (with CD's) and go to the strip (road where the bars and clubs are located)

---

* a resort destination on the South-Eastern coast of Cyprus synonymous with British ravers and influential for supporting early UK garage and grime

and hand them out to people.' He acknowledges Ayia Napa, a known clubbing hotspot, for housing part of the crossover of UK funky house. 'I remember when I first went there in 2009 a lot of people from various uni's were out there and a lot of the raves were purely funky raves. A lot of the MCs were out there like Gracious K, Funky Dee, Trilla, who was huge in Birmingham, but I didn't know how huge until we were in Ayia Napa.' Larizzle adds, 'I've never heard Gracious K's Migraine Skank so many times in a day!'. He goes on to speak about the impact of the beach party culture on the clubbing Island, 'I felt like it really helped cement the UK funky sound and helped to elevate those big multi uni linkup raves as well.'

The genre's versatile ability to defrost the iciest of screw faces and stush* attitudes created an infectiously positive atmosphere, as Larizzle recalls, 'the ladies would sing along to songs by Egypt, Princess Nyah and Kyla, but I remember those really hard-hitting instrumentals would get people gassed, and when the MCs would spit their known bars, that would take it up to another level.' The impact of those early women-led songs such as 'Frontline', the Drake-sampled 'Do You Mind' and Katy B's 'Tell Me' helped UK funky cross over to the mainstream with catchy hooks and melodic instrumentals.

When you strip it back, UK funky house recognises pre-programmed polyrhythms through drums on digital software. The sound and community it emerged from represents genres of the past and the present. Within the defining age of UK funky house, early hints of Afrobeats were present, Larizzle recalls one track in particular where this is clear. 'There was a track by Apple called 'Mr Bean'. That was one of the first underground funky tracks I heard. I was like Whoa... what is that?!' I asked him what attracted him to the song. 'It was drums. Mainly Bongos actually. There were some synths in

---

*   uptight, judgemental attitude

there as well. It was just different and it was slightly slower than garage but it had this energy. The bass was insane.'

UK funky house, like Afrobeats, shares a sense of home-coming. The emphasis in both genres was placed solely on the music as opposed to being spread across fashion, postcode wars and macho bravado.

It was about 'enjoyment' or as many of my peers would now say 'h'enjoyment'. The copious amount of skanks* that would accompany the brilliant instrumentals would be an important part of UK funky records. Some tracks ranged from feel-good party anthems like Kyla's 'Do You Mind', Egypt's 'In The Morning' and Attaca Pesante's 'Make It Funky For Me' to novelty public health awareness songs like 'Catch It. Bin It. Kill It'. The skanking culture of UK funky house was intrinsic to the genre. It's a sentiment Larizzle affirms as a fan first, 'it was all about skanking and just energy through limbic movements. It was a good time…any opportunity I get to take it back to that time now I always take it.'

As we speak DJ Larizzle reflects on time with the Mista Silva a decade earlier, 'we did loads together back in those days and it felt like a bit of a family. He would throw a lot of Ghanaian ad-libs into his bars.' Larizzle also references other key MCs in Coldstepz and Ramzee (also of Ghanaian descent) who had the infamous reload bars** of 'whose dat lightie' and 'unite da rave up'. Before we end our insightful conversation, DJ Larizzle speaks on the camaraderie built through their shared heritage and good energy. 'There was Essex Uni in Colchester…there was a ridiculous lineup of DJs and MCs. When it came to the funky set, there was about ten MCs. The energy was just rising with the instrumentals.' He adds with

---

* the precursor to TikTok dances usually uniting ravers moving to the same anthem as one in unison

** familiar lyrics from an MC or artist which would send the rave into pandemonium particularly in a call and response fashion

the hint of a grin, 'It was always good to combine some vocal tracks with a few instrumentals…It was almost like teamwork where an instrumental would be riding and we would gauge the crowd synonymously. If we ever saw it waning, we would pass the mic to that MC who would have that bar which would bring back the energy.'

CONCLUSION

Afrobeats as a younger sibling to UK funky house is the archetypal symbiotic relationship in the development of Black music in Britain. Switching between English and the mother tongue via Patois and Pidgin in everyday speech and song reflects the greater cultural influence of the West African migration in the UK. For a new generation proud to display their multiple identities through emoji flags on their social media bios, the music from the uni rave era provided an unapologetic and joyful bedrock on which to celebrate African heritage, planting the seeds for the sonic growth of Afrobeats via the crossover efforts of acts like Donae'O and Fuse ODG.

7

IS IT REALLY
EVERYDAY DANCE?

Dance in African society and the wider diaspora has origins in storytelling. It is an expression of life itself. Dance for 'us' allows the improvised movement of the body to represent a wider examination of things like social class, oral history and major life milestones. Anyone of African heritage will have early memories of recreational family gatherings that served training grounds for performance in this informal capacity. Quite simply, African families dance together and do it often! They do it in their living rooms, in their churches, and in their hall parties. The joy of dance is a natural bond shared between African kin far and wide. In many ways, for us, it almost like another language.

Our first memories of dance tend to be when we were young, wide-eyed and without inhibition. When it came to the language of dance in an African household you fell into different categories—'the trier' who had the will of a dancer but would shake with the rhythm of a blocked condiment bottle, 'the professional', who somehow came out of the womb as though they had a nine month sabbatical at the Juilliard school of dance, 'the motivator', who yelled ad-libs more than they danced but their screams distracted you from noticing they never really danced and 'the one' whose fluid organic dance moves would electrify the dance floor and leave fellow dancers gaping in awe.

The lineage of African dance is wide and far-ranging. When we zoom in on West Africa, we find like many other regions in the continent, the language of dance is an ancestral history lesson. In my case, this history lesson takes shape in the Adowa dance. Originating from the Asante tribe in Ghana, the Adowa dance is a traditional and social ritual regularly performed at funerals, festivals and other public events in Ghana. It's a movement which not only reflects the obvious physical communication but also the oral history that reinforce the status quo and influences on wider society.

The Adowa dance is usually performed by women, though my brothers and I would morph into rare anomalies as we were thrust into the centre of the dance floor. Aided by my mother, the matriarch (herself of Asante royalty) and flanked by our more respondent younger girl cousins, my brothers and I would dance the night away.

Usually at Diversity Day, which was a day where children from different nationalities could celebrate their parent's heritage unapologetically, we wore traditional Kente and confidently stepped into the primary school hall.

Rhythm and our relationship to it is a hugely important part of how we as Africans interact with our culture. It is not always a smooth relationship and in some cases it takes many years of being pushed into the centre of the dancefloor before frantically running through the fire exit in embarrassment. For some of us, before we are comfortable dancing in front of our peers and family members we grow into our rhythm in solitude. We watch our bodies accept their rhythmic calling in the comfort of our bedroom or toilet mirrors (this was certainly true in my case).

In *The Music of Africa*, the late renowned musicologist JH Kwabena Nketia explores dance and offers his theory on its relationship within African society. He recognises that whilst music can carry meaning through its message it can also create a stronger sense of unity. In the West, dances from Africa have been painted with a brush of exoticism in large part due to the perception of the Black African bodies that house the dances. The clear Africanness of these dances and their proximity to pre-colonial Africa frame them alongside archaic 'voodoo' stereotypes.

Popular music of Black origin and its relationship to the West follows a cycle of subordination and censorship. The Caribbean, with its many islands and open influence from European invaders from the 15th to the late 17th century, was the counterpoint and epicentre for a menagerie of colonial influence from France, the Netherlands, Spain and Britain. Oral communication on plantations in the Caribbean was forbidden and slaves were subjected to a horrific level of labour in unbearable conditions, alongside the inevitable abuse from plantation owners.

In Trinidad, in particular, this context would form the backdrop to the early embers of the Kaiso genre in the early 17th century, which would later evolve into calypso as it was an early example of African slaves crafting a way to describe their struggle at the hands of their oppressors. The music was used as a uniting force across the Caribbean region, playing an important role in the processes of confrontation, revolution and revival.

A look into the origins of the Calypso tradition sees the original name 'Kaiso' originating from the nomadic Hausa tribe of Nigeria. The movement itself, a mixture of West

African and French Creole which came about through chant-wells*. It was usually men who performed this role and were viewed as early calypsoians who held the oral history of those of African origin in a new setting. The verbal language reinforced the Kaiso dance as a form of empowerment to reinforce your sense of identity and imagine what a home away from your ancestral birthplace looks like.

In the West Indies, dances still exist to this day that are influenced by polyrhythmic drumming and African spiritual traditions.

As a medium, dance is emblematic of the response to lived experiences. It is an expression of the Black body releasing emotion, preserving the past in the present through movement.

J.H. Kwabena Nkatia explores this through his view that through dance people are able to display how they feel in relation to others. For Nkatia, dance is a soothing act which can solve any problem between individuals and rivalling groups. A dance can be used as a form of respect and appreciation to well-wishers. It's one I have seen readily played out at parties and funeral celebrations where a gift is given as an offering and the one hosting the occasion will play a requested song to show gratitude.

Dancing as a response to drumming styles and the particular rhythms played would serve as an identity marker for what tribe you came from in West African culture. Dance is also used to express courtship, celebration, fertility, spirituality and religion.

One of my earliest childhood memories is attending church as a toddler. I remember watching as I grasped my mum's hand as the church band played percussive medleys backed by the clapping of the congregation. As an adult, I think fondly

---

*   another form of griot, an African storyteller usually of an elder persuasion who would preserve the traditions of the tribe

of these all-night church sessions which started around mid-night. They were like a free rave replete with good music and good company. In recent times, gentrification has taken its grip in areas dominated by Black Africans such as Tottenham in North London and Peckham in South London. The influx of a middle-class white population along with property developers using buzzwords from the 'diverse-tionary' threatens the existence of safe spaces that have been cultural hubs for Black communities.

A 2017 article in the *Evening Standard* titled, 'Entrepreneurs: Baby's sudden arrival wasn't even a stretch for yoga couple' looks at a influx of hipsters* who set up a yoga studio. According to the article, these hipsters would soon complain about their gong baths being disrupted by the sound of Sunday church worshippers in the Bussey Building in Peckham. 'There were about 20 West African churches in here… There'd be massive ghetto blasters and screaming,' says the [redacted] new hipster. The statement is… well, I will leave you to decide how you want to describe it. But clearly this individual did not research the demographic of local residents in Peckham. The article, once you push past your initial shock, lays bare a pressing issue regarding Black communities in the capital and other cities alike.

The African church presents one of the last safe frontiers where African congregations can express their religion through the medium of praise and worship. In a city which can often feel hostile toward Black joy, the pushback the few Black spaces receive is worrying to say the least.

---

* Cultural chameleons usually of middle to upper class status who congregate in working class areas of cities now touted as 'edgy' and 'vibrant'. Easily distinguished through their coffee consumption and wearing knitwear irrespective of the weather season.

Dance in African culture is a language that enjoys freedom and true inclusivity. The shy and stiff spectators are just as welcome as the most impressive of dancers. It's a pattern that enables the continual gift of choreography to organically develop over a wide-ranging timeline. Dance has been a consistent and central part of West African music pre-Afrobeats. So, as one would expect, dance remains equally integral in contemporary Afrobeats. Just as the continued borrowing of polyrhythms and melodies exist within Afrobeats, dances have similarly been borrowed and developed within the new genre.

Dance in Afrobeats and generally West African music is about agency and how individuals choose to express movement in response to sound—it is this agency that often makes this kind of dancing look as though it is completely improvised. The structure and evolution of the polyrhythm into the modern context of African music will be touched upon in a later chapter.

For now, let us reflect on the fact that dancing within West African traditions are sets of visual and physical reactions to music. The visual and physical reactions originate from historical rituals from various ethnic groups within West Africa. A notable one, is the formation of a circle around a newcomer as a welcoming act. Here there is no hierarchy, there are no boundaries between spectator and dancer. It's a communicative relationship where the collective rhythm built by foot stomps, hand claps and the beating of the drum builds a sense of solidarity and strength.

THE EXPLOSION OF AFROBEATS DANCING

Toward the start of the previous decade, the first wave of Afrobeats on the continent came with a strong dance element. If there was an Afrobeats song, you could bet your bottom naira that there would be a charismatic dance that accompanied it. Afrobeats dancing became the courier of the music and this marriage would lead to the creation of a new industry—the Afrobeats dancing industry. The development of the Afrobeats sound intersected with the height of the social media boom in the mid-to-late 2000s. This meant that almost all had a camera phone and almost all had a social media account—this provided a vehicle for new African dances to travel into untapped markets.

Afrobeats dancers became a commodity, using twitter, instagram and youtube as their means of communication. Out of this boom came Afrobeats dance classes, online dance challenges, and viral moments. The online world of Afrobeats dancing became its own international entity with dances racking up millions of views on platforms like youtube and facebook. These videos would come in many forms, including but not limited to, impeccable and professional choreography, humourous dance parodies, endearing dance imitations and many more. Another interesting element was the location and environment of such visuals. These dance videos were recorded anywhere and everywhere including dance studios, parks, bedrooms, schools, buses—much like the freedom of the dances themselves, there were no restrictions to who could participate and how they could do so. At the peak of the Afrobeats dancing boom (which one could argue is still occuring) everyone was dancing and everyone was recording it!

Afrobeats and its dancing fused with the height of the

social media era pushed the dances out into the world. Part of the fast success of this dancing was that you had an international African diaspora who were able to lock in to dance challenges and trends, from all over of the world. Now, this idea of the internet providing a global market for a cultural trend or movement is not a new concept, but when we think about it in terms of music originating from Africa, it is something that West African genres like hiplife, highlife and Afrobeat (without the S) never had access too. Thus, the development of this modern sound and its language of dance meant that for the first time an 'African' sound (Afrobeats) and expression (the dance) had the international world at its fingertips.

AZONTO

Originating from the Kpanlogo dance, the Azonto is a free-flowing highlife dance form performed to conga-like drums and music of Ga heritage in Accra's historical Jamestown community. The Azonto is a seminal dance that followed the lineage of the Kpanlogo move from the 60s to the present as a form of expression for young people in Ghana.

It's a communicative full-body dance which involves hip and knee movements along with hands, shoulders and arms open for improvising. Its interpretation has been refined by seasoned dance pros and freestylers.

The transnationalism of the dance occurred in large part because of the internet. The dance would be a massive facilitator between Africa and an inquisitive first generation community of young Africans born and raised in the UK. This was accelerated by Ghanaian rappers Sarkodie and E.L's song 'U Go Kill Me' produced by the 'originator' Nshona Musick in 2011. A simple piano riff supported by a swirling synth bass and arresting drumbeat, would provide pockets of space that made the track perfect for the azonto movement to interject.

A year later, British-Ghanaian artist Fuse ODG released a song called 'Azonto' (which would later be officially released in October 2013). This song would firmly place the dance at the epicentre in the United Kingdom. British-born and of Ghanaian descent, Fuse ODG took ownership in terms of popularising the dance beyond Ghana in late 2011 with renowned Ghanaian producer Killbeatz at the helm. Proclaiming before the start of the song, 'I've just come back from Ghana and I wanna share this dance that everyone was doing over there.' The original video details two dancers in black tracksuits rocking hoodies and wearing white masks to cover their faces. The two dancers proceed to azonto-ing by iconic landmarks in the London's West End.

The song features established Ghanaian artist Tiffany, whom over the second verse of the song switches from a fake American lilt to fluid Twi—a reflection of the bilingual code switching present in Afrobeats. Towards the end, Fuse and Tiffany's musical interplay acknowledges an appreciation for dances that serves as glue to keep those of African heritage connected to the motherland.

Currently the music video has racked up over 34 million views (and counting) on YouTube. Its crossover appeal is even more powerful given the societally relentless routine in the UK where young Black people are demonised for wearing tracksuits and hoodies, which the two dancing stars of the music video adorn unapologetically.

One of the hooded and masked dancers in the video is a man named KB (Kwabena Benko). KB would become a figure who was heavily featured in the first wave of UK Afrobeats.

KB speaks about the early days of dancing over a crackly phone line in late Spring 2019, 'I used to go to parties and it used to be hiplife and highlife… I used to dance and they used to splash me with money.' Like many children of West African migrants, the celebratory West African party setting strongly informs KB's relationship with dance. The party setting would also provide KB with a creative outlet where his religious upbringing did not support his enthusiasm for dance. KB explains, 'I am a SDA (Seventh Day Adventist), so growing up in church it was very hard for me to dance as they looked down on dance… we mostly sing hymns.' An adage that can be traced back to the western missionaries in West Africa disliking dance as a form of praise for early converts.

'Dancing was something which always made me happy' After KB's early years in his homeland of Ghana and a brief period in South Africa, he moved to the UK at the age of 14 to join his settled father. He remembers the hostile cultural environment within the UK at the time, one that was influenced by cultures from across the Atlantic, which made it difficult for a young second generation KB to fit in. 'I was very fresh, the way I spoke meant that I used to get picked on. Most people [wanted to] be Jamaican and they never wanted to claim they were African.'

His father's support and determination for KB to find strength in his heritage would manifest through a chance meeting with another dancer Selasi at the popular Gold Coast club in Brixton. KB reminisces fondly about the venue (now permanently closed), 'I used to go with my friends…I am the type of person who likes to dance when I go to parties. At that time, I was more of a freestyle dancer but I said let me give it a go.' KB goes on to explain how his official entry into the Afrobeats dancing wave began: 'I saw a video of him [Fuse ODG] on Instagram, he has released a new song called Antenna… We saw it as more than just a dance and wanted to tell a story with what we were doing. So me and Selasi (did a video and the response was amazing…that's how it all started.'

Early Afrobeats music videos were similar in this sense. They would often feature young African schoolchildren in the UK in their uniforms effortlessly freeing their limbs at lunch-time. Smartphones and social media were used to archive the explosion of Afrobeats dancing in its first wave in the UK. After the positive viral response to the Antenna Dance Challenge, KB and Selasi would later perform with Fuse ODG regularly.

American writer and ethnographer Jesse Weaver Shipley explains the Afrobeats dancing internet phenomena: 'As digital signs become markers of authenticity, the proximity to home becomes less important than the ability to be inti-mately Ghanaian anywhere.' Shipley articulates perhaps one of the most significant elements of the spread of the Afrobeats dancing and consequently Afrobeats culture as a whole. The internet allowed Africanness to exist without borders and spread faster than ever before.

When KB returned to Ghana to perform with FUSE ODG in the 2000s, he was impressed with the virality of the genre's dancing, 'I was in Bojo Beach (near Accra) dancing and a few East Asian people approached me. I was amazed and wowed… and started teaching them the basics of Azonto.'

KB's love for and success within Afrobeats dancing would eventually lead to him creating his own dance company called Move With KB.

KB was not the only dancer who was able to contribute and build within the world of Afrobeats dancing. HomeBros were an influential dance duo of Ghanaian heritage. The pair were individually known as Uncle TC and Kurty. They were born and raised in East London and trained in various dance styles first honing their craft training at award-winning dance company Boy Blue in the UK.

I meet the pair close to their ends in a floating eco-friendly hotel with The O2 arena in our view.

The childhood friends both attended Brampton Manor Academy (formerly Brampton Manor School), the second largest secondary school in the London Borough of Newham. The school's sixth form at the time of writing the book is one of the top academically performing schools in the UK for Black and minority ethnic groups.

Uncle TC and Kurty Swift note the diversity of student intake from across the borough during their time at the school. They explain that this fostered a strong sense of community. As Kurty Swift says, 'that was one thing that was cool for us lot in Newham as we could still go to many areas without really being stressed out because we knew people from before their life changed.'

Both men note the impact of the second wave of the hiplife genre, referencing seminal tracks such as the song 'Shordy' by Ghanaian rap trio Praye and 'Abuskeleke' by Ghanaian artist Nananom Sidney'.

Uncle TC remembers the experience of listening to music at hall parties. 'You are expecting to hear songs and when the DJ didn't play it you would be like oh! As we started to get more comfortable dancing, there were tracks that I would wait for so that I could go off on the dancefloor.' Kurty Swift chimes in, 'it's way better than anything I have heard musically. Some of these songs aren't even quantized and they are played live off the cuff. For me one of the times where I knew that our sound was heavily superior was when DJ Neptizzle used to DJ at our family hall parties.'

HomeBros entry into university in 2011 coincided with the start of their journey with Afrobeats. Like many students of West African descent at the time, attending Afrobeats nights became a large part of one's nightlife. Over time they would become facilitators of this university Afrobeats scene and eventually they would get booked for events. Kurty Swift reminisces about their swift elevation within the university Afrobeats rave circuit, 'we started [university] in late Sept/ early Oct, Fresher's Week, all of that. By January, was when we released our first video and it went viral, so by the time it hit February… people weren't looking at us like these young guys who go [to] uni.' Uncle TC adds a regular utterance they would hear in their university days 'You man are from YouTube… You're the dancers!'

HomeBros would soon go on to dance in the music videos for early UK Afrobeats classics, such as Mista Silva's song 'Boom Boom Tah', Fuse ODG's song 'Antenna' as well as a tutorial video for Tribal Magz's 'Tribal Azonto'.

HomeBros would take ownership of this dance craze that was bubbling, eventually hosting dance classes for those curious about Afro dance styles.

One example of this shift has been where artists premiere their track in dance classes. Afro B's Joanna in particular was an example of this where the artist himself attended a class and played the song for the HomeFam (the name given to the dancing community which the HomeBros have built). The launch of the subsequent #drogbachallenge currently stands at over 200k views featuring one of the HomeFam dancers (@prinnyc_ aka Courtney Yao) flexing to one of the most successful crossover Afrobeats tracks in 2018.

Freestyling and improvisation is a central part of Afrobeats dancing. It is part of what makes the expression of African dance so freeing and limitless. On the topic of freestyling within Afrobeats dancing Kurty Swift explains, 'that's what we call "going missing." It becomes an unconscious freestyle whereby you have no idea what you are doing, what you are going to do… you are just going and it's just you and the music. Sometimes it looks like people are glazed over like it's a high moment.' The vulnerability that comes with putting the ego aside in this physical manifestation of music is something Uncle TC articulates well: 'you are just trying to find a place… where everything else is gone and it's just you and the music, being in your own spirit in the music and using dance as an expression. If you get to the point where you can feel, it's the purest form… so for me dance is feel.'

Kurty Swift explains, 'it feels like your ancestors are pushing you especially when I dance these Afro-dance styles because there is so much culture and heritage behind it. You feel like your ancestors are saying, "Well done. Go!"'

With a vision to pass on dancing and culture to the next generation of upcoming dancers within the African diaspora, legacy and heritage is key for HomeBros. 'We are changing perceptions,' Kurty Swift explains. 'Everyone is doing their part to try and change the perceptions of Africa in their own ways.'

SKELEWU

Recorded and released with an instructional dance video in August 2013, Nigerian musician Davido's hit 'Skelewu' would become the next big West African dance anthem. In a way the song became the Naija rival to the Ghanaian dance and name-sake song of 'Azonto'. 'Skelewu' was a sweeping Afro-pop song with a subtle trance-like soundscape with European house pounds. It was a forthright example of engineered marketing meets ready-made musicality. Davido, understanding the potential for the dance to go viral, uploaded an instructional dance video to accompany the song. The video was laidback with Davido and his boys nonchalantly standing on cars with arms flailing. The dance consists of rolling shoulders back-wards with one arm facing forward and the other placed on your waist (not too dissimilar to the 'Nae Nae' dance). Skelewu itself is a title derived from Nigerian Pidgin and means 'being deceived' in English. It aligns with the opening lines 'All the girls them dey dance galala/but this new dance don cause casala'.

The official music video would be released in October 2013 and captures the infectiousness in a dystopian London street setting, emphasizing once again the genre's reach and the strong link between Afrobeats and the UK. The video features a humorous interaction between Davido and a young Black British boy who is attempting to resist the addictiveness of the song. Set far away from the dance's choreographed conception in Lagos, the London video features dancers of all backgrounds adding their own twist to the dance.

The song would be nominated for Song of the Year at the 2014 MTV Africa Music Awards and was a viral hit thanks to the brilliantly engineered social media dance competition. 'Skelewu', like many other Afrobeats hits after it, was a prime example of how having a dance accompanying an Afrobeats song would do wonders for its success and reach.

YAHOOZE

One of the early Afrobeats songs that infiltrated the UK ACS rave circuit was Nigerian musician Olu Maintain's song 'Yahooze' released in 2007. The chorus cry of 'Yahoo' and response of 'Oh Oh' brought an accompanying dance calling you to make a V sign with index and middle fingers (like peace signs), swaying them into the air. The Yahooze dance derived from the bravado of fraudster males known as 419er's who would indulge in flamboyant lifestyles. The song title of 'Yahooze' itself comes from 'Yahoo', which was the email account that 419er's would scam unaware victims from.

The YouTube comment section of the music video is filled with humorous and nostalgic posts such as one user commenting, 'every African Londoner must know this song!' and another posting, 'it took me 13 years to realise this was about scamming people.'

ALKAYIDA

A younger brother of the aforementioned elder Azonto, is a dance known as Alkayida. This was another effortless movement originating from the Ghanaian capital of Accra in 2013. Its early beginnings rose amongst schoolchildren in JSS (Junior Secondary School) and the dance soon gained popularity with the release of the song 'Alkayida (Boys Abr3)' from hiplife rapper Guru.

The song title would go on to attract controversy for the overt link to the widely known terrorist organisation Al Qaeda. Backended by traditional percussion in a slow tom-tom drum and pan flute opening to give it a folk essence, the sparse synths and Atlanta stomp drums make the song a memorable anthem. The dance itself has two stages involving a gentle swing of the arms across the waist as they cross with each lean in one direction and the opposite hip in the other. The other stage consists of a Fat Joe-esque lean back motion and rolling the chest with arms comparable to the stagger after carrying a heavy crate of drinks.

Readily incorporated into Azonto moves in a freestyle capacity and even repurposed by spiritual pastors using the dance in Sunday services, the Alkayida is another important counterpoint for Ghanaians at home and inquisitive dancers abroad.

SHOKI

An inviting dance move that emerged from Nigeria in 2014 is the shoki. Its origin is within Agege, a neighbourhood located in Lagos, Nigeria. Agege is a settlement that was formerly the centre of thriving kolanut plantations. The plantations attracted the majority Yoruba tribe, who favoured the minority Hausa tribe's skills as labourers to cut the trees of the popular snack.

The dance's popularity can be traced back to yet another self-titled track, 'Shoki' by Nigerian musician Olamide's protege Lil Kesh, and was released in 2014. Colloquially known as 'quickie', a rough translation of its Yoruba origins, the Shoki asks the dancer to raise their hands up open-palmed toward the sky and then to drop their hands with their palms facing downward. It's akin to an NBA player nonchalantly throwing a three-pointer on the court.

The 'Shoki' song was subsequently banned by Nigeria's National Broadcasting Commission months later in an attempt to censor the sexually suggestive nature of the song and its accompanying dance. 'Shoki', is a Nigerian Pidgin word, one that was used in the epoch of Fela Kuti and King Sunny Ade in Afrobeat meaning, 'well on point and direct'. The subsequent remix to Lil Kesh's song would feature Davido and Olamide a few months later and the dance's popularity would rise with over ten million views and counting.

The Shoki dance would soon go back to Agege with its own festival called The Shoki Festival in 2015. The festival's mission statement was 'Celebrating Your Origin', a statement that speaks to the sentiment of the wider Afro-prefixed musical sound. The prominence of that dance, however, did not end there. The influence of the dance would grow again, specifically in the UK, when the Team Salut produced song

'Dance For Me' by British-born artist Eugy and Mr Eazi was released in 2016. Eugy's refrain of 'shoki/mi se alkayida and dab' fluidly incorporates the popular dance moves in the music video for the song.

Three languages are sung in the song's chorus, including Yoruba, Akan and English. With English as the official language uniting many across the African diaspora the Shoki dance further cements close relations between Africans in the continent and beyond.

SHAKU

Perhaps one of the most well-known dances within Afrobeats is the 'Shaku Shaku'. Another dance originating from the Lagos sprawl, it was formerly known as 'Jaku Jaku'. In the recent *Idunu Taxi* music documentary from visual collective Crudo Volta, the charmingly animated, goldie-lock-haired Nigerian musician Slimcase speaks about the origins of the Shaku dance in reference to a local madman who first performed the dance.

The dance holds an adaptability that has caused many well known African artists to imitate it in songs and videos. The Shaku is used by Nigerian superstar Wizkid in his song 'Soco' and is featured in Nigerian artist Naira Marley's unofficial Super Eagles[*] World Cup anthem 'Issa Goal'. Afro B would release a song called 'Shaku Shaku' featuring regular producer collaborators Team Salut in 2018, which as you can guess is a homage and celebration of the dance. When it comes to songs that featured the Shaku in their choreography, the list really does go on. The dance has since become an intrinsic part of modern West African culture.

The dance is one taken in stages with the left foot stomped

---

[*]   Nickname for the Nigeria national football team

down and the right hand pulled back akin to an experienced archer who doesn't have to look at this weapon. The same move continues concurrently on the other side of the body until both arms cross and meet in the middle. Similar to the communicative vein of the Azonto, the pulled back arm sometimes transforms into a telephone to speak and attract a resonant listener on the floor. The dance would soon reach a unique nadir with Liam Payne of One Direction who was taught the dance in Ghana in 2018.

ZANKU

The most recent dance to catch viral fire in the aftermath of the annual Homecoming, a cultural mini-festival inviting those of Nigerian and African heritage back to Lagos, Nigeria in December 2019 was the Zanku. The Zanku was first witnessed in Nigerian artist Chinko Ekun's song 'Able God' featuring Lil Kesh and Zlatan released in 2018. Chinko Ekun along with Lil Kesh and Zlatan dance the Zanku in the regal church setting.

The Zanku is closely affiliated with Nigerian artist Zlatan Ibile through his own single 'Zanku Legwork' released in October 2018. The official music video showcases the dance's accessibility with a diverse group from toddlers to young adults waving white handkerchiefs through the arms in the motion of a wind-up radio ready to spread energy.

The Zanku is a dance where the arms are crossed towards the hips with your back arched like a T-Rex. The hands must be swaying side to side in tandem with the legs gently bouncing horizontally before the release of the leg kick.

The birthplace of the dance is once again from Agege. The official purveyor of the Zanku, the artist Zlatan, has made an acronym of the name , 'Zanku Abeg No Kill Us'. The dance's popularity increased with Zlatan's Burna Boy collaboration on the Kel P produced 'Killin Dem', released in 2019. The choral lyrics of 'Popopo Popopo Popopo' serve as the simmer before the boil of the lyrics, 'Gbese, Gbese gbe soul e'. Both translate into English as 'lift your legs' and 'lift up your soul'.

8

THE SONIC CREATORS: MUSIC PRODUCERS

The shift in music formats from the physical to the digital often leaves music purists bemoaning the lack of quality in the present day package—whether that be the way music is distributed or the quality of the sound. We have all heard someone say, 'vinyl just sounds better'.

Whatever your opinion is on the format of music today, when we look back to the good ol' days of the vinyl, one perk were the inner sleeve notes. These unassuming paper sheets would open your eyes to the number of people behind the scenes that helped an individual artist or group. Session musicians, studio locations and mixing engineers are some of the roles which come to mind. Not to forget arguably the key component behind the artist—the ever so valuable music producer.

Across music of Black origin, the drum is often a key instrument in the communication of music. The drum is the rhythm, it is the foundation. In the scope of colonial and post-colonial Blackness, the drum represents the retainment of identity despite slaves stolen into new lands in North America, Europe and the Caribbean. We see this through the history of calypso via griots and the chanting in Trinidad. The centrality of drumming crops up again in the Rastafarian tradition of Nyabinghi drumming. Nyabinghi drumming is the rhythmic bedrock for ska, rocksteady and reggae, and a myriad of music that followed Jamaica's golden era of dub. The accompanying music itself is a blend of 19th century gospel music and African drumming.

Today drumming is felt amongst Black communities in every possible setting—the Church, music festivals, the club, hall parties, cookouts, carnivals, day parties. The drum is a musical lineage which binds many Black musical expressions together and transforms Black strangers into long lost siblings on the dancefloor.

As explored in the Burger highlife chapter, African migration and technological advances in the West during the late 70s would affect the next wave of West African genres that would soundtrack the 80s and 90s—some of which were Nigerian disco boogie, Burger highlife and hiplife. These musical expressions would in turn provide new projections for what it meant to be African with Western sensibilities. It would be during this transitional period that live instrumentations such as drums and horns would be swapped out for drum machines and synthesisers. The sounds that came from this period have been routinely misinterpreted by middle-class journalists and DJs who have reduced the sonics to funk and disco without correctly acknowledging its clear and unapologetic Africanness. This sonic Africanness would be created by trailblazing African music producers such as Nkono Teles, Lemmy Jackson, Bodo Staiger and Bob Fiscan.

When we speak about music and genres generally, we often centralise the artist and don't shed enough light on the huge contributions of music producers. This chapter will attempt to represent a number of influential and rising producers that retain African sounds in their music, whilst pushing and developing the African sonics like never before.

The first Azonto wave in the early Noughties gained

further popularity when the Ghanaian men's football team known as the 'Black Stars' famously celebrated their goals with the dance in their run to the quarter finals of FIFA World Cup 2010 in South Africa. This would be the first time the world's most watched sporting event was held in Africa. The 'Black Stars' former captain Asamoah Gyan was also an artist under the stage name 'Baby Jet' and regularly performed the Azonto after scoring a goal.

Michael Gafatchi, known as Gafacci, is a versatile producer with Ga roots from the La area of Accra, Ghana. He is the son of Sega Gafatchi, a revered and talented Ghanaian musician who was previously a key part of Nigerian artist Chief Ebenezer Obey's band as well as the late Tony Allen's Afro Messengers band. Gafacci's musicality is grounded in traditional jama and kpanlogo drum (a type of barrel drum usually played with two hands) with electronic manifestations inspired by asokpor music, a Ghanaian genre that is a fusion of 90s house and percussive sounds. In recent years we have seen Gafacci move into the European club scene with remixes for the likes of Swedish electronic act Fever Ray and Portuguese producer Branko's Enchufada label.

Gafacci would go on to produce Kpokpo O Body (Shake Your Body) released in 2011 by Dee-Money featuring D-Black. The song has a stop-start bounce, military tom roll and tension-inducing soft synth strings. It was well-received and saw Gafacci's popularity rise among young Ghanaians and migrant communities in the diaspora. I finally meet Gafacci in the flesh amidst the humid sun in Ghana in December 2019. We break bread over pizza at a popular globalized chain in a mega mall.

As we dug into the pizza, I asked him about his earliest musical memory: 'There was a church beneath our house...

I would go into the church and sing with them… they would even call me to the front and I would be dancing.' With the initial aspiration to be an artist, a young Gafacci would soon leave for education. His introduction to the cult music software FL Studio (also known as Fruity Loops) would soon see him advising studio producers on the ways to arrange beats.

Gafacci, like many great musicians, attained his musical influences from a mixture of places. On the subject of these influences, he explains, 'I was heavily into stuff from Texas [and] Atlanta. I grew up an outsider, as in Ghana, the Western music which was big was East and West Coast and I was South.' Gafacci's love for Southern hip hop and American trap would exist alongside his love for Ghanaian hiplife. Interestingly, Gafacci would lean into producing music that had a different sound to these influences and would create club-orientated riddims. In 2011, Gafacci would produce the song 'My Kinda Girl' by D-Black featuring the Ghanaian O.G Sarkodie. Despite the song being nearly a decade old, it does not sound dated and speaks to Gafacci's musical foresight. His unorthodox approach in collaboration pushed his production away from a saturated market in Ghana and would soon see him find another portal that allowed his experimental roots to travel even further.

Gafacci would continue to develop his sound, producing a copious number of instrumentals which would resonate with the ears of East Midlands hailing DJ and producer Murlo. In 2017, Gafacci officially released the breakout song 'I Like Your Girlfriend' featuring fellow Ghanaian rapper Bryte on UK based label Ransom Note Records. The song is an upbeat anthem that clearly upholds its UK funky house influences. Gafacci states that, 'UK funky was big in Ghana (2010) and one of the influences is Donae'O's Party Hard. You would hear Funky Dee, Lethal Bizzle and Tempa T.'

As he lists a number of British-Ghanaian artists and their musical impact within Ghana, I ask him why he thinks London based MCs were so popular in Ghana, Gafacci responds noting the impact of travel on slang. 'It's like £600 to come to Ghana at a very good season and there are a lot of Ghanaian communities in the UK. The music, fashion, phonetics, into-nation…' Interestingly, he draws my attention to a song by Ghanaian artist Tiffany, named 'Fake London Boy'. A song that was a satirical take on people from London.

Gafacci didn't readily find musical allies in Ghana due to his own vision and thoughts on the popularity of Afrobeats. He explains, 'maybe people had thoughts about what I share with them (musically) and I realised no it's just in my head. I will go and (try to) experiment with music and it worked.' In the early 2010s, his different approach to musical production would place him in a unique position in part due to how his dual listening experience from the UK and USA informed his music and outlook.

During the height of the Azonto's dominance in the UK I stumbled upon a young producer on Soundcloud whose African Crates Volume 1 mixtape sampled vintage Ghanaian highlife and Nigerian Afrobeat from the halcyon era of the 60s and 70s. This producer would upcycle them into hip hop instrumentals, not too dissimilar from the African-American canon, taking jazz breaks a la J Dilla on the MPC Drum machine. Born Julian Nicco-Annan to Ghanaian migrants in Hackney, this producer is now better known as Juls. Juls is without a doubt a significant player when it comes to the course of Afrobeats with his influential partnership with artist Mr Eazi. Juls's parents moved to the UK in the 1970s and were music aficionados of genres like jazz, reggae and highlife. A young Juls would be taken to concerts regularly by his parents and was immersed in the musical environment because of them. Juls's early exposure to live music led to him developing a studious interest in music with the initial grounding from his elders.

In 1996, Juls's family relocated to Ghana and it was here, whilst studying at the University of Ghana, Legon (the oldest university in the country) in the mid-2000s, that he would experiment with his own musical production.

In the early 2010s, Juls would send a CD of instrumentals to Nigerian hip hop group Show Dem Camp via Ghanaian musician Efya. One of the tracks would become the Show Dem Camp song called 'Feel Alright' released in 2012 featuring Poe and Boj of Nigerian group DRB Lasgidi. The song provides a gentle highlife guitar and minimal percussives blended with electric kickdrums in the background.

'Teef Teef', from 2016, follows a similar sonic formula with Ghanaian artists Eugy, Sarkodie and Mr Eazi all switching between Pidgin, Akan and English backended by 808 drums. It would be Mr Eazi's connection with Juls that would assist him in developing an initial Afro-pop sound.

They initially connected over Mr Eazi's About To Blow mixtape with 'Bankulize' from that project being remixed by Juls featuring Italian-Ghanaian artist Pappy Kojo, a measured song with gentle bass guitar and smooth keys. An early prequel to Banku Music, a term popularized by Eazi as a fusion of Ghanaian highlife and Naija juju. This blending of sounds owes to time spent in Kumasi, Ghana, for school. The dancehall and R&B flavoured 'SkinTight' featuring Efya and 'Anointing' filled with the Yaa Asantewaa leaning riff and Daddy Lumba gospel chords not only enhances Eazi's musicality further but heightens Juls as a facilitator.

Juls's production is infectious for many reasons, one being his ability to create cultural potency through the use of live instruments. Much like those who came before him Juls is a master of blending the digital with the traditional, the new with the old. His music continues to retain a sense of home and heritage whilst also being rooted in contemporary culture. These sentiments are very much reflective of not just the Afrobeats movement but also the continent of Africa itself, a key emerging market that is developing rapidly societally and economically.

The versatility of Juls's production can be found in songs like, 'Like Tu Danz' featuring Pa Salieu, Ms Banks and Kida Kudz (from Colour), GoldLink's 'U Say' featuring Tyler, the Creator and Jay Prince, the soulful Soweto Blues with Busiswa and Jaz Karis and the recent transatlantic collab EP Fufu & Grits with Mid-West producer Sango channeling Brazilian funk, Afrobeat and amapiano.

Despite the fact that Black women's contributions are valuable and often the source, we find that time and time again they exist in artistic industries that relegate them to the background. In the context of Afrobeats or African music this is no different. One woman in particular that has navigated this industry and excelled is the powerhouse Karen Nyame aka KG.

Hailing from North-East London, Karen Nyame is a producer and DJ of Ghanaian descent. Nyame's journey into music was rooted in curiosity. At the young age of 8, Nyame would take deep interest in demo CD's from glossy electronic music magazines, leading her to explore new genres that she may have not been otherwise exposed to at that age.

Nyame grew up in a household where her parents played a mixture of ballad rock, Motown and highlife. She recalls the sound setup in her first home: 'my parents kept playing on a big sound system… part of the decor you know! My Dad would invest in [Notting Hill] Carnival amps. We're on the third floor! There are neighbours!'

Curiosity and creativity combined in equal measure to develop an ear for all types of music.

Her second hand musical experience by way of her parents was an early baptism in understanding sound quality. Speaking on this time in her life, she explains, 'I feel like that was the moment I connected with melody and emotion even to the point where my aunties, cousins and my cousins knew.'

Karen Nyame, like many children of West African descent (including myself), has distinct memories of hall parties: 'I am just picturing the dresses my Mum used to put me in. The drip* was very serious. We dress up just to sit down and watch our parents dance. Can you imagine all of this dressing up for no reason?' The hall party is a mutual and early reference point binding the West African experience in the West.

Nyame divulges more about her hall party experience and laughs when I name the Broadwater Farm Community Centre in Tottenham as a hot spot. 'Broadwater Farm is Accra (capital of Ghana),' she explains. 'That hall! The small one every time whether it be from the funerals which are more celebrations... Birthday parties... It's just the commemoration of Ghanaian culture at its finest. It was a point of connection even though we're in Britain right now we are always going to find a way to reinforce the fact that this is home now'.

KG's peers would develop practical skills in the playground where they would MC over garage beats and listen to local pirate stations like Deja Vu and Mystique Radio. This would be something KG would regularly emulate through her own music production on the school computer. 'That is where most of my musical influences were birthed from even though I am multigenre.'

Karen Nyame almost fell out of love with music after a teacher accidentally deleted Nyame's Music Technology

---

*   dress sense

coursework in College causing Nyame to consider studying Broadcast Journalism instead. Luckily for us, this was not the case and musically this period would be a seminal moment for Nyame, 'Uni was when I came to my first introduction to broken beat and UK funky,' Nyame states. '[It] has a more polyrhythmic African energy to it. When it comes to UK funky , every rave I would go to at uni people were just taken by the sound. I was like okay I need to get in on this.'

In 2009, Karen Nyame would be inspired by the university rave scene and craft the single 'Feeling Funky'. The track 'Feeling Funky' would then be remixed in 2010 with Nyame's vocals on the song along with artists like Tribal Magz, Sway and Sarkodie repping Ghana and the UK. Nyame goes on to to say, 'you know the layers in which African music embody. It's just the power. It's spiritual. An element of euphoria even in soulful house tracks.' She adds, 'the emotiveness behind that and the antithesis on the flipside is the aggression and I found that UK funky embodied the two. You would hear 'African Warrior' and 'Devil In A Blue Dress' and it would evoke the same type of feeling.'

UK funky was a unifying genre with an encyclopedic range of chants and dances. The raves of the university scene were much like the hall parties we attended as children two decades before.

Karen Nyame's musical exposure and ability has given her the percussive pulse to create space and move forward via Afro-bass and gqom* music in the present.

Karen Nyame has also released music on heavyweight record label Hyperdub collaborating with UK producer Scratchclart (fka Scratcha DVA), an O.G. of the underground

---

*   Originating from an onomatopoeic Zulu word signifying a drum, it's an electronic subgenre from the townships of Durban, South Africa

scene yielded the *Touch* and *The Classix* EPs released in 2019.

'I am very very African and don't get it twisted,' Nyame says. 'We have to be grateful for all the musical resources we have here, which allows us to submerge and push into musical worlds where it's not common for maybe Black women to command space in the dance music world'.

Often unheralded, the producers of the hiplife genre in Ghana particularly those of the second wave in the late 90s to early 2000s provided the instrumental backbone to the sound. At the start of each song, a producer's tag via an ad-lib or a sound effect prior to the commencement of a song affirmed ownership of production. A subtle and at times overt reminder before the lyrics kick in that the producer shares equal status with the artist, who will inevitably gain most of the adulation.

Jeff Tennyson Quaye better known as Jay Q was a key producer in the popularization of hiplife introducing rhythms via the cowbell instrument, drums and hand claps from the jama tradition (an uptempo pastime originating from Ghanaian secondary schools and football fans), amongst other traditional elements. His signature bottle breaking sound would be the prologue to production for regular collaborators Buk Bak, VIP, Castro and classic highlife artists Daddy Lumba and Ofori Amponsah. Like many sound technicians, the Church was an entry point to Jay Q's love of music. Jay Q played on a drum kit and was on the Conga drums at the Emmanuel Assemblies of God Church in Accra whilst studying music and the keyboard at the Oriental School of Music.

A meeting with studio mentor Fred Kyei Mensah—himself a prolific facilitator who worked extensively with Ghanaian artist Daddy Lumba—exposed Jay Q to the new school of musicians in Ofori Amponsah at the Fredyma studio. Mensah taught Jay Q music programming and introduced Jay Q to recording. With the dawn of a new millennium and digital recordings on the rise, Jay Q moved from an analog studio in CHM Studios using software Cubase and Notator on an Atari computer to Virtual Studio, a fully digital recording studio in Accra. It was a fertile base in which he helped foster the careers of artists like Buk Bak and VIP. Buk Bak was a group who represented an audio antithesis to the majority of Twi-speaking artists with drum patterns of Ga origin fused with lyrics in the Accra-based dialect through songs such as 'I'm Going To Come' and 'Chingilingi'. As explored in Chapter 4 Hiplife—Fusion and Culture, the group VIP would build a gradual following in the mainstream with a solid youth fanbase.

However, it wasn't until their fourth album *Ahomka Wo Mu* released in 2003 alongside the popular title track of the same name that they received more acclaim, staying No. 1 in Ghana for over 20 weeks. The song 'Ahomka Wo Mu' is an intergenerational classic riddim. The song has even been sampled by Nigerian rapper Kida Kudz and Birmingham artist JayKae on the track '1am' allowing Jay Q's legacy to live on with a new generation two decades later.

With the Covid-19 pandemic, social media provided a unique opportunity for music lovers to get to know music and musicians in unique ways. The Verzuz series created by American producers Swizz Beatz and Timbaland opened up artist discographies and allowed ownership of the narrative bereft of any PR team or music label.

A Ghanaian equivalent of Verzuz arose under the name of Behind Da Hitz where the aforementioned Jay Q went head to head with another influential Ghanaian producer in Appietus. Born Nana Appian Dankwah, Appietus's signature hook of 'Appietus In The Mix' can be heard on the back catalogue of many hiplife compilations. Appietus would go on to forge strong musical relationships with an array of African artists across genres. However, it would be his relationship with Ghanaian artist Ofori Amponsah, and the late Castro, that would cement his position as a true stalwart of the Ghanaian sound. Ofori Amponsah in many ways was the natural heir to Daddy Lumba after dropping out of school to work under his guidance. Amponsah's R&B-esque and Afro-pop style would soon be heard on bangers like 'Broken Heart', 'Odo Nwom' (sampled by UK artist Tion Wayne and One Acen on '2/10' produced by Diztortion), 'Emmanuella' and the seminal classic 'Otoolege' (featuring K.K. Fosu, Barosky and Kofi Nti). Arguably one of Appietus's most played hits, the love for 'Otoolege' is reflected in the comments under the video, where several YouTube users profess that, while they lack an understanding of the meaning of the lyrics, they still resonate strongly with the sonics.

In recent years, Appietus has managed to keep his prolificacy as a producer despite branching off into mentorship and acting. Though he is not crafting with the regularity of his prime, his production on two tracks allowed him to add his flavour on the Azonto wave. These songs would be Ghanaian trio 5Five's song 'Move Back (Muja Baya)' and Sarkodie's 'Azonto Fiesta'. 5Five's 'Move Back' would cross-over into the wider diaspora with its original sample lifted from South African artist DJ CNDO's song 'Amerido'. Appietus added a further grand piano refrain and British-Ghanaians Mista Silva and A-Star, along with the duo Kwams and Flava, bringing with it a new generation. Appietus' career has provided a classic musical catalogue that has pushed sonic boundaries for over two decades.

In the last decade, a South London-based producer of Nigerian heritage has made his mark on the Afrobeats scene. Hugely influenced by his Church upbringing and growing up in the UK's capital, P2J (also known as Pro2Jay) has seamlessly blended Afrobeats and dancehall to create a sound that has crossed the diaspora and has resonated further with Stateside artists. Like many West African children, P2J's early connection to music can be traced to Church where he would go every Sunday with his family. His household was also filled with the music selection of his parents where they would play a plethora of classics from Motown to Bob Marley. P2J's mother in particular would introduce him to Nigerian artists such as King Sunny Ade and Fela Kuti who would later become key inspirations in P2J's musical journey.

I finally receive some WhatsApp voice notes where P2J recalls his early musical experimentations 'I used to go to a Catholic Church. There was a choir and they used to make us sing every Friday. I think that was probably the first bit of music I started making.' He adds, 'I started writing harmonies for the choir when I was ten. It was a kids choir and we used to sing loads of stuff for Sunday Service and from there I just started writing songs for myself to see if I could write.'

These experiences would inform his versatility in his early career, producing with Channel U grime classic 'Hands In The Air', UK funky banger Fr3e's 'Tribal Skank', and early UK Afro-pop in Lola Rae's 'Watch My Ting Go'. These songs were a roll call of riddims that personify P2J's attempt to hone his style, he reflects on the impact of the latter two songs. 'When I made 'Tribal Skank', I just wanted to do something different at the time so I dived into it trying to make it sound as African and funky as I could. That's the reason why there is some Yoruba dialect in that song. I tried to draw some grooves and textures from Afrobeats music and add it into funky house.' He continues, 'the Lola Rae song was a different approach as it was more of an Afro-pop vibe and it's something which I had never really done before and it was an experiment and from then it gave me a platform to try new vibes and just grow as a producer. I feel like the funky house song ['Tribal Skank'] definitely gave me the leverage to start making Afrobeats as that was the first song which gave me the bridge into the Afrobeats world.'

It's a transition which has since proved fruitful, as he now regularly works with the Afrobeats triumvirate of Burna Boy, Wizkid and Davido in the studio. The former in particular he first met whilst engineering a session for him and the two would strike up a rapport that would see the producer make his first tracks in 'Koni Baje' and 'Devil In California' for Oluwa Burna on his third studio album *Outside* in 2018. The following year, P2J produced party starter 'Anybody' from the critically acclaimed and Grammy-nominated *African Giant*, released in July 2019. P2J explains the process behind the hit single and what it's like to collaborate with a global superstar: 'I started the beat the day before we linked up not knowing I was going to link up with him. I went to the studio and we were supposed to do something else and at the time he was like let's make something fresh real quick.' He adds, 'I just pulled up the beat which was just the groove and the chords. He then said, "yo let me go in the booth." He did one take of melodies and bam the vibe was created. He started writing lyrics to it and 'Anybody' was formed. In post-production, I just added some special instruments like the sax, the bass and just gave it the full vibe.'

P2J's work has extended further than African artists, credited as an executive producer on US artist Goldlink's debut studio album *Diaspora*. The album was a soundtrack that aimed to unite Black people across the Black Atlantic through rhythms from Africa and the Caribbean. P2J's contribution to the album in many ways is an organic consequence of growing up in London where Afrobeats and dancehall have blended. The album saw Goldlink relocate to the UK capital and understand more about the sounds that reflect the city's Black population. The simultaneous release of the Beyoncé-curated *Lion King* album *The Gift* a week earlier that same month in July 2019 would finally see P2J arrive onto the American stage. At the helm, he produced and co-produced six songs on the project, including 'Brown Skin Girl', which became a Black women's empowerment anthem. P2J reflects on working on the album: 'the *Lion King* process was an amazing one. It was difficult and very challenging trying to get the vibe of the film and the vibe of the project. It was a challenge that everyone was up for.' P2J further adds, 'my favourite memory was probably in Jamaica when we started 'Brown Skin Girl'. We started four ideas and we landed on 'Brown Skin Girl' towards the end of the session. It was a big vibe and a special moment.'

Nearly a decade after an initial trip to break into America, P2J's dream for African music to crossover to the mainstream has come to fruition. After executively producing Wizkid's *Made in Lagos* album, he acknowledges, 'I am happy that the world is now hearing and feeling the energy that deserves to be heard.'

9

AFROBEATS
(YES, WITH AN S)

In my younger days, Sunday evenings were the purgatory between the underworld of the weekend and the zombie march of the school week. There I was, right before bedtime, scrambling to complete homework two and a half days before the deadline. During this time in my life, British drama and factual shows were solely primed for Middle England (notable ones included, but were not limited to, *Last of The Summer Wine* and *Heartbeat)*. In these shows there was not a even token Black person in sight. For me and my peers British television did not really speak to us bar the odd show here and there. We did, however, find a home in another medium. The radio.

During the same time slots as the middle England shows (or their reruns), there was a show called *The Afrobeats Show* airing on Black British radio station Choice FM. It was hosted by a young Ghanaian-British DJ called Abrantee. The show, for me and many others like me, came to be one of the most important shows we listened to. *The Afrobeats Show* played a key role in elevation of African music across the diaspora, and would become an entrenched feature in the lives of the many young African diaspora listeners.

Choice FM was Britain's first licensed station playing music of Black origin non-stop. Founded and launched in 1990 in Brixton, London by Patrick Berry and Stuart Reed. The radio station was a hub of Black music within the UK and became a safe space for Black British music as well as international Black music. It would be in April 2011 that a young DJ called Abrantee would launch what would become known as the *The Afrobeats Show* on the station. *The Afrobeats Show* would air weekly equipped with Abrantee's zeal for the sounds of west Africa.

Alongside DJ Edu who had his *Destination Africa* show on BBC Radio 1XTRA that first aired in April 2005, DJ Abrantee would be an early facilitator of the emerging Afrobeats sound in the early Noughties.

In 2019, the government of Ghana rolled out an initiative called the Year of Return, to welcome and encourage those of African descent back to the African continent via Ghana. During the Year of Return, the cultural impact and influence of DJ Abrantee's radio show was shown in an interview clip between Abrantee and US artist Jidenna, in Ghana. Jidenna asserts to DJ Abrantee, '[Afrobeats] goes around the UK, Europe, the world and then America, which really pushes it… complete circle because of you.' He added further, 'I believe you were one of God's pivotal soldiers… for you to do it is a sacrifice of body. You did it to give music to people to spread the music around the world so we have unity between the diaspora and the continent.' A testimony full of praise from an African-American artist of Nigerian heritage who found an initial safe space in the UK on DJ Abrantee's show.

Afrobeats as a term is one that stimulates expansive dialogue whenever it is brought up. All you have to do is log onto twitter and see the many threads debating and disputing who coined the term 'Afrobeats'. Many media reports credit DJ Abrantee with coining the term 'Afrobeats', but the truth is this is not always agreed on. The Google Ngram Viewer, (an online search engine that charts the use of words and phrases in sources printed between 1500–2019) shows the term Afrobeats appears in sources as early as the 1980s though its appearance was minimal. As one would expect we find that in the 2000s the term Afrobeats appears much more regularly, peaking in 2019 where the chart ends. The truth is we may never discover who coined the term Afrobeats and to be honest, as a lover and self-professed child of Afrobeats, I am not sure it really matters. What we do know is it is a term derived from the term Afrobeat, coined and created by the late and great Fela Kuti.

Defining Afrobeats at times is an impossible task. Some push away from labelling such a phenomenon, others have different opinions on what it is, but for the most part it is agreed that Afrobeats is an evolution on Fela Kuti's Afrobeat developed in the 2000s. Over time the word has become an umbrella term for contemporary West African music or con-temporary West African styled music, one that fuses multiple genres together, some of which include Afrobeat, hip hop, dancehall, hiplife, R&B, pop, highlife and rap. Whilst there is a distinction between Fela's Afrobeat and Afrobeats, both are centred in the pride of African heritage and what it means to African.

When we attempt to pin Afrobeats to a location it becomes even more interesting. Without a shadow of a doubt Africa is the centre, more specifically West Africa, but when we assess where it crossed over first and what locations propelled it further, we find that a little city called London played a rela-tively significant role.

The UK Afrobeats scene is one that emerged from mul-tiple Black subcultures. These subcultures specifically pertain to the young Black working class community. In 2019, British researcher Jessica Perera produced a background paper, 'The London Clearances' for the Institute of Race Relations. The report states that, 'young BAME communities in London have responded to this socio-economic exclusion from mainstream society by creating strong subcultures which provided meaning to their lives and firmly established their right to live in the city which they have helped to fashion.' Perera further adds, 'these young people often associated with grime, road rap and drill… have come to collectively encapsulate a way of life for disadvantaged young Black people trying to navigate their way through intersecting forms of oppression.' Within this urban framework, UK Afrobeats has provided an organic connectivity to Africa through the post-colonial thread of the English language, the official language in many African countries. There is a bitter reality in the fact that English, a language that was violently inflicted on many African countries, has now become a vehicle for people of African heritage all over the world to share their musical musings and expressions. However, as we have explored throughout the book, it is the Africanness of the music that is at the essence of Afrobeats.

Another important and unsung thread of Afrobeats is the intersection of sport and music, in particular, football. Within the African diaspora, the world's most watched game has contributed significantly to the growth of Afrobeats in the last decade. If you're a football fanatic by proxy of heritage or just a curious aficionado who regularly watch 22 people chasing a leather sphere on a green rectangle, then you too may be aware of the marriage between African football and African music. The African Cup of Nations also known as the AFCON is regularly viewed by the eyes of managers and the British media.

AFCON is a unique departure from the typical muddle of domestic football competitions.

It is a tournament that is a reflection of Africa as a continent and not one that relegates African countries to the sidelines. It provides a space for African countries to reflect the nuances of their region unapologetically on home soil. It is for that reason its popularity is both important and radical. Music plays a huge role in this tournament from binding players and fans with Ghanaian praise songs in the jama style, a feature personified via the Ghanaian men's football team, who you hear before seeing them enter a stadium pre-match. Other notable nations whose celebrations of coordinated choreography in the past have brought the tournament to life include Cameroon, Uganda, South Africa, Nigeria doing the Soapy dance made famous by Naira Marley's song of the same name. Equally memorable is DR Congo doing the Finbu, a Lingala word referring to a type of whip, which was once a symbol of Belgian colonial violence in the central African nation. Today it has been repurposed as a playful gesture, insinuating the whipping of opponents. It's a dance which accompanied the Congolese pop hit also named Finbu by Felix Wazeka. These celebrations often give a sense of humanity and build a greater connection to AFCON fans at home through the medium of music.

Interestingly, in 2007, UK rapper Sway released his *The Dotted Lines Mixtape*. Born Derek Andrew Safo in North London, Sway was an early role model with his versatile, witty and laidback flow. The cover of *The Dotted Lines Mixtape* has Sway in black and white in the foreground with the red, green and gold colours of Ghana proudly behind him. His stance in the middle of the cover is deliberate with the rapper presenting as the black star (the sign at the centre of the Ghanaian flag). Perhaps the most popular track on the mixtape is a song called, you guessed it, 'Black Stars' which provides a beautiful homage to Ghanaians in the diaspora.

Now known as Sway DaSafo as opposed to his original rap moniker, Sway's love for Ghana was a harbinger of things to come. His musical career would see him perform and support Ghanaian hiplife rappers such as Sarkodie and Tic Tac, which assisted in bringing these acts to prominence in the UK.

London has provided a fruitful ground for Afrobeats in a way that did not and perhaps could not occur in other Western cities. Historian Marc Matera notes the UK capital's historical significance pertaining to Black culture and expression as early as the 1920s: 'The imperial metropolis became an important node of the circuits traveled by Black musicians and Black expressive cultures, facilitating musical exchange, the creation of innovative hybrid forms, and expansive visions of the African world.' He adds, 'Black musicians in London, predominantly a mix of British-born, Caribbean, and African subjects of the empire, self-consciously combined Afro-Atlantic forms, expressing in another register solidarity and mutual influence within an interconnected Black world.' Matera's assessment can be applied to the reggae movement within the UK, the development of grime music and now Afrobeats.

In *The African Diaspora Population In Britain*, Aspinall and Chinoya note the Black African population in England and Wales was almost a million larger than Black Caribbean and other Black groups combined. In the last 20 years in the UK, music has continued to serve a vital function, for children of West African heritage. A direct result of their parents', and in some cases their own, migration to the United Kingdom from West Africa, the idea of being Black and British is no longer solely focused on the cultural impact of the Caribbean islands on British society. The growing Black African population in the diaspora openly take pride in their heritage seeking cultural references back to their roots and London. In this sense London is the home of Afrobeats outside Africa.

This cross-continental continuity is found when two Nigerian men arrived in London in the early 2000s. One hailing from a family heavily influenced by a military father and religiously devout mother. Whilst the latter was firmly involved in music, playing traditional and percussive instruments from a young age. Oladapo Daniel Oyebanjo and Michael Collins Ajereh better known as Nigerian artist D'Banj and Nigerian producer Don Jazzy both worked as security guards in the UK, an assimilative entry point for many uncles from West Africa attempting to make sense of their new surroundings.

Whilst working their 9-5's, the two men were simultaneously pursuing music. Their pursuit of music would eventually bring them together initially through mutual friends and subsequent sessions in the recording studio in 2000. It's a union that resulted in the creation of the seminal Mo'Hits Records label after they both returned to Nigeria in 2004.

Don Jazzy would become the CEO and President of the label with D'Banj as the co-owner and becoming the first artist signed to the label. D'Banj's early singles 'Tongolo' from his debut album *No Long Thing*, released in 2005, and 'Why Me' from his second studio album *Rundown Funk U Up*, released in 2006, found minor success within Africa.

'Why Me?' would go on to win the Listeners Choice Award at the MTV Africa Music Awards in 2008, a whole two years after its initial release. However, it would be D'Banj's third LP titled *The Entertainer* that would finally see him cemented as a bonafide performer. It is possible that the album release of *Curriculum Vitae* from the Mo' Hits Allstars (a music group comprised of Don Jazzy, D'banj, Wande Coal, D'Prince and K-Switch) in 2007 gave D'Banj the confidence to be more open in providing feel-good music for the masses.

In an interview with Don Jazzy for the Nigerian Newspaper *Vanguard* in 2011, he highlighted a shift in marketing which contributed to the triumph of *The Entertainer*. Don Jazzy reflected, 'if I want to release a single now, I don't just put out one single. We wait for the videos and put it up.' Don Baba J (another alias for Don Jazzy) added, 'from the time of D'Banj's 'Entertainer', I put out three songs like 'Gbono Feli Feli', 'Olorun Maje' and 'Too Much'. These are markets for both the Yoruba, Igbos and others. 'Gbono Feli Feli' was for the club. 'Olorun Maje' was more gospel. 'Too Much' was more like a gambling song.'

D'Banj's signature move of positioning the microphone around his crotch with suggestive traits are reminiscent of the hypnotic movements of artists like James Brown and Fela Kuti. D'Banj's blend of Pidgin English, Yoruba and English permeates his records comparable to his aforementioned role model in Fela Kuti. The opening track of *The Entertainer* is 'Gbono Feli Feli'. The track is a bold and boisterous assertion of D'Banj's manhood with lyrics like, 'I'm hot/you're not,' and the further refrain of, 'don't hate me/cos' I'm better than you.' The shuffling drum backbeat echoes the early era of The Neptunes—think Britney Spears's 'Boys' with added classic arpeggio keys and a warped synth.

The critical and commercial success of *The Entertainer* was a landmark moment for African music. D'Banj's musical success would make it on the radar of a superstar from Chicago called Kanye West. This would result in a crossover moment for Afrobeats whilst also triggering the start of tensions between D'Banj and Don Jazzy.

With a large and growing fanbase back home in Nigeria, D'Banj's artistry now began to invite interest from abroad. D'Banj would often frequent London, where he found a natural and loyal fan base. The pinnacle of his success in London was his sold out show at the Hammersmith Apollo in 2011. The highlight of the sold out affair involved a stage cloaked in darkness whilst D'banj played a harmonica to

Kanye West's hit 'All Of The Lights'. What went on to occur was an early international display that was not yet common for Afrobeats. The bass drops and the lights flood the stage, then the moment of the night happens —Kanye West himself arrives on to the stage and the crowd go wild.

D'Banj would soon be signed to Kanye West's GOOD Music record label, an announcement that Kanye West would make on stage that same evening. Shortly after the performance of 'All of the Lights' Kanye West would take off his Gold Yeezus piece and place it around the neck of the D'Banj. It was quite the moment—here we had one of Africa's golden boys stood side by side with one of America's golden boy in a fashion that was never seen before. Today, we look back at this moment as an indicator of the future global terrain of Afrobeats.

The following year in 2012, amidst the Summer Olympics spectacle in London, the global focus was on the city like never before. The same year D'Banj would release arguably the most easily recognisable Afrobeats song to date 'Oliver Twist'. Initially released in May 2012, the song entered the UK Singles Chart at number nine and was the first Afrobeats song to chart in the UK top 10. The music video featured a number of cameos from across the diaspora in an empty studio purporting to be a rundown, red brick house featuring the CEO Dancers group, David Vujanic and Eddie Kadi to name a few. D'Banj's use of the fictional Dickens character was a device to ask for more women, in his case referencing notable Black women.

In the first verse, D'Banj mentions Beyoncé, Nicki Minaj from the African-American side and then takes it back closer to home with African Movie Stars in Genevieve Nnaji and Nadia Buhari.

A year prior to the song's official release its underground

popularity in the UK via its initial ascendancy in Africa resulted in it being the first track played after the midnight countdown for London's New Year's Eve celebrations on the River Thames, an event that draws in millions of viewers every year. According to Afrobeats promoter Bankuli, 'it was also the bicentennial celebration of the Oliver Twist book.' This level of pre-promotion soon saw the song trend on Twitter. D'Banj's success with Oliver Twist would lead to major labels finally taking notice of home-grown British stars who had already established their own Afrobeats subculture, which would serve as a catalyst for the wider African diaspora a decade later.

An individual who himself embodies a personal history that follows the emergence of Afrobeats is Michael Ugwu. British-born of Nigerian heritage, the former General Manager of Sony Music West Africa has played a pivotal role in the development of the Nigerian Music and Entertainment industry. I first came into contact with the North-West London-bred entrepreneur in the early Noughties. At the time, Ugwu was the CEO at iROKING, an online digital music platform focused on West African labels and artists. Launched in December 2011, iROKING was the first musical platform of its kind taking an interest in cataloguing and representing the musical nuances that were coming out of the region. This is all the more staggering when you consider Western streaming counterparts in Spotify and Apple Music still had yet to launch in Africa.

During his tenure at iROKING, Ugwu also oversaw the signing of over 50 of Nigeria's biggest artists including Bracket, 2Face, Timaya and Duncan Mighty to landmark licensing deals. Over a classically delayed WhatsApp call owing to distance and intermittent Wi-FI connection, I managed to speak to Michael Ugwu in early Spring 2019. I first query the juxtaposition of the rise of Afrobeats with the digital potential of global music distribution. He responds by reflecting on his earlier times at iROKING and the challenges they faced, 'We did the economics and [it] just didn't work at that time… We wouldn't have been able to digitise and then recoup from streaming revenues in Africa alone.' His honest assessment reveals a frequent downside of being the first to do something in an untouched industry, nevertheless Ugwu's passion to aid Nigerian music remains.

As we speak further, I touch upon how music reaffirms a sense of duality amongst first and second generation Africans within the diaspora. 'It is definitely changing the perspectives of young West Africans internationally, highlife with the contemporary. It gives a picture we are somebody and we come from somewhere. This is our culture. This is who we are.' He speaks on Afrobeats music as a timeline of experiences between the traditional and new. 'I was always in-between… I think what the music has done on a historical and contemporary level it has connected a lot of dots for people who may not feel quite sure where they are coming [from] and where they are going to.' Ugwu had early role models from the Nigerian music scene in Plantashun Boiz, Olu Maintain and Styl-Plus to name a few. He stated, '[Also] I adopted Mo Hitz, Wande Coal… This became our own [scene]. The Afrobeats without an "s" belonged to our parents. So we always appreciated [it] for what it is, but now and where I sit in the music industry is about the contemporary scene.'

Ugwu is aware of the dominance of Nigeria owing to its large population and big communities in the diaspora: 'I think the Nigerian artists have been at the forefront as the Nigerian diaspora is quite big and it helped the early artists like 9ice and D'Banj but now the other artists are coming in. I think it's great as it keeps everybody on their toes with regard to the scene and how the scene penetrates the mainstream where the most value is being derived from.'

'Afrobeats at the moment… It's a whole movement right now. It's kinda uniting the diaspora… [It's] good music, it makes you want to move, want to dance, it's feel-good music with African percussions as well. The feeling that you get from it is just different.' A glowing statement made in mid-2012 by FUSE ODG in a Youtube interview, FUSE ODG has long held an early passion for Pan-Africanism in musical form. His early tune titled R.W.A.N.D.A uses the East African country as a positive acronym standing for, 'Really Wise And Never Doubts At All', which was FUSE ODG's attempt to subvert the typically negative associations of warfare and genocide readily attached to Africa. This would be a precursor to his T.I.N.A movement; another acronym that stands for, 'This Is New Africa'.

FUSE ODG's early singles such as 'Billy Elliot's Black' (featuring Mikel Ameen), 'A Song For Libya (Find A Way)' and 'Mama I'm In Love', are all examples from his early discography of a young Black man attempting to figure out his place within a country where Black identity is often treated with hostility.

However, despite minor underground success within the university confines of ACS societies and music circuits. It wasn't until FUSE ODG took a trip to Ghana at the start of the early Noughties and linked up with Ghanaian producer Killbeatz that a fuse was lit (pun intended).

It would be FUSE ODG's early studio sessions with Killbeatz in 2011 where he would witness people doing a particular dance to the music played. The distinct dance was infectious and memorable—it was none other than the Azonto dance. A manifestation of movement that would soon be transported from Accra to the UK through FUSE ODG's self-titled song 'Azonto'. In writer and researcher Jesse Shipley's 'Transnational circulation and digital fatigue' paper, written in 2013, FUSE recalls the motivation behind the creation of his cult hit, 'it (the dance) was uniting people… Everyone was teaching me... how to do azonto.'

As mentioned in chapter 7, the song and dance was a cultural explosion within Accra initially and soon spread to London giving the Azonto greater prominence in the West.

'Nobody wanna see you rising/and when you do they don't even like it/They just wanna see you deep in crisis, drive yourself, you don't need a licence.' The song sends a universally empowering message about pushing oneself through struggle irrespective of the haters. It is an archetypal feel-good anthem.

After the initial underground release of his 'Azonto' song, FUSE ODG signed to 3 Beat Records, an independent British record label. Another more polished music video for 'Azonto' was released in October 2013. The new music video came with cameos from DJ Neptizzle, a bleach-blonde-haired Tiffany and a last additional verse from a fresh-faced Donae'O. Towards the end of the new video a white man responds enthusiastically to FUSE ODG, gassing up his interpretation of the Azonto dance, a sign of the song's ascendance into the mainstream a year after its initial release. FUSE ODG's single 'Antenna' was similarly coupled with a dance challenge that went viral and gave Fuse another hit in June 2013. Antenna would peak at No. 7 on the UK Singles Chart.

FUSE ODG released his debut studio album *T.I.N.A (This Is New Africa)* in October 2014. The album would feature the singles 'Azonto', 'Antenna', and 'Million Pound Girl (Badder than Bad)', which would peak at No. 5 on the UK singles chart, and 'Dangerous Love', which would peak at No. 3 on the UK singles chart.

In an April 2019 interview with Tim Westwood, FUSE ODG reflected on his album *T.I.N.A.* He said, 'I did 'Antenna', which was Afro-dance, I did 'Million Pound Girl' which was Afro-bashment.'

The latter song was one centred around the empowerment of women, something that FUSE ODG took outside of music with his own line of African inspired toys called 'Nana Dolls'. With the tagline, 'Little Queen with Royal Dreams,' each doll is dressed in traditional Kente cloth with a contemporary twist and named after a inspirational African woman including Nehanda (Zimbabwe), Kuti (Fela's mother), Makeba (South Africa) and lastly Yaa (Ghana).

The sound of FUSE's single 'Million Pound Girl (Badder Than Bad)' would be one of the earlier success stories of West African musical style mixing with Caribbean style, a fusion that is now a dominant force within the UK Music scene and abroad.

In the interim of *T.I.N.A.*'s success, the surprise release of FUSE ODG's single 'Boa Me', with superstar Ed Sheeran and Mugeez (one half of the seminal hiplife and Afrobeats duo R2Bees), took both FUSE ODG's profile and the profile of Afrobeats even further. The Twi[*] title translates to 'help me'. Produced by Killbeatz, the song has Ed Sheeran singing in the Twi dialect. Interestingly it would be the same studio sessions that created 'Boa Me' that would produce Ed Sheeran's song 'Bibia Be Ye Ye' (Everything Will Be Fine) from his Grammy Award winning LP ÷ *(divide)*, released in 2017. Fuse ODG would be a credited writer on the song and Killbeatz would

---

[*]   a dialect of the Akan language

be an accredited producer on the song, resulting in them becoming the first Ghanaians to ever win a Grammy.

'I really appreciate you. But I don't appreciate the way [my] name is written so small in your bill. I am an AFRICAN GIANT and will not be reduced to whatever that tiny writing means. Fix things quick please.' This is a statement taken from an Instagram post made in January 2019 by the now Grammy award winning Nigerian artist Damini Ebunoluwa Ogulu better known as Burna Boy. The caption was a response to the flyer of the 2019 Coachella music festival where Burna Boy was set to perform. At the time of this confident statement Burna Boy was not as decorated as he is now. His critically acclaimed, grammy nominated album 'African Giant' released July 2019 was not yet released neither was his 2020 Grammy award winning album 'Twice as Tall' nevertheless Burna Boy's assertion symbolised how he viewed himself and his music.

In some respects, his statement points to something bigger than him, almost a call for the international world to put some respect on the name of African music. Shortly after his Coachella annoucment, his career would skyrocket. At the time of writing this book Burna Boy's music has captured the imagination of wider global audience all of whom acknowledge his ascendance as one of the most well known artists from the African underground scene to crossover into the mainstream.

Burna Boy comes from a musical family. His grandfather Benson Idonije previously managed the legend Fela Kuti and serves as Burna Boy's Director Of Music to this day.

Burna Boy would attend high school near Lagos, Nigeria, before moving to London in the late 2000s. However, it would be upon his return to Nigeria that his music career began to take off in 2012 with the release of his song 'Like To Party'. A track flowing with open, hedonistic expressions along with the vices of alcohol and women. The song produced by Nigerian producer Leriq personifies Burna Boy's early confidence riding European trance synths with laid back R&B drums.

Burna Boy was another early example of an artist who fused African sonics with Caribbean musical style. His debut studio album *L.I.F.E.*, an acronym meaning Leaving an Impact For Eternity, was released in 2013 on Aristokrat Records. The album's cover art had a childhood photo of Burna in traditional agbada* holding a microphone with glee. In the background there are faint outlines of Bob Marley, Fela Kuti and King Sunny Ade looking over a young Burna Boy.

'Boom Boom Boom', one of the first tracks of Burna's discography, takes the 'I never tell you finish, I never tell you finish' line from Fela Kuti's 1972 song 'Lady'. On the album was also Burna Boy's single 'Tonight' which was dancefloor ready with swinging dance synths taking the lead in the vein of a 90s house classic. In the song Burna Boy blends English, Yoruba and Igbo. His reggae and galala**-inspired song was informed by inner city Lagos. The song was a huge hit amongst the African diaspora abroad and in the continent, being a regular addition to university rave playlists. Burna Boy's attempt at producing a memorable record for the Afrobeats canon would see his debut album *L.I.F.E* enter the *Billboard* Reggae Albums chart at a healthy No. 7 in August 2013.

---

*   a full formal attire usually decorated with intricate embroidery, and is worn on special religious or ceremonial occasions in West Africa and the diaspora

**   a dance form originating from the ghetto areas of Nigeria and popularised in the 90s by pseudo-reggae musician Daddy Showkey

Following this initial success, Burna would soon leave Aristokrat Records in 2014 and release his second LP *On A Spaceship* on his independent record imprint Spaceship Entertainment. The most notable banger on the album was 'Soke', an afterparty nocturnal anthem. Importantly the song cemented Burna Boy's ability as a musician able to commentate on the social realities in Nigeria. In the song's music video, Burna Boy walks around still members of the public as he speaks on their behalf.

All of this would culminate in Burna Boy's 2017 move to major label Atlantic Records. With this signing came a shift in Burna Boy's collaborations, which were previously the likes of home-grown West African brethren such as Sarkodie and Skales. Now in what seemed to be a new musical phase, Burna Boy began creating music with artists like J-Hus, Lily Allen, Fall Out Boy and Major Lazer. *Outside*, his third studio album released in 2018 entered the *Billboard* Reggae Albums Chart at No. 3 in February 2018. The album featured the song 'Sekkle Down' featuring the music powerhouse J-Hus with production from Jae5. Another song, 'Heaven's Gate' featuring Lily Allen, is another standout feature on the album with Burna flowing effortlessly between Patois and London slang. However, the most notable song on the album is reserved for the last single release from *Outside*. Simply known as 'Ye', the song is spiritual, uplifting and onomatopoeic in its iteration. Unbeknownst to listeners at the time, the song and style would be a preview of what was to come in arguably his most critically acclaimed album *African Giant*. The song has become one of Burna Boy's most well known songs and crossed over to other markets attaining 11 million streams over seven months on U.S. streaming platforms. The song won Song of the Year at The Headies 2019 in Nigeria. It also won Song of the Year and Listener's Choice at the 2019 Soundcity MVP Awards Festival in Nigeria and is guaranteed to shut down raves and parties every time it is played.

Burna Boy's stock continued to rise and he was named as YouTube's Artist on The Rise and Spotify's Afro Hub Takeover Artist in October 2018. Both platforms noted Burna Boy's versatility across continents and what he represented for African musicianship.

In the *Artist Spotlight Series* documentary on YouTube, Burna Boy remarks, 'Most of the things that have shaped me into the man I am [today] are what London taught me.' His statement highlights the centrality of London in the life of one of the biggest Afrobeats artists of our time, which mirrors London's centrality in the success of Afrobeats itself. Burna Boy's passion to follow his dream as a musician is given deeper meaning when looking at his family. Not only is Burna the grandson of the legendary manager of Fela Kuti, but just as Fela Kuti's mother was hugely influential in Kuti's life, Burna Boy's mother plays a pivotal role in his music career. The powerhouse that is Bose Ogulu also known as Mama Burna is the mother of musician Burna Boy and doubles up as his manager.

The arrival of Burna Boy's fourth studio album *African Giant* released in 2019 signalled another phase in Burna Boy's music. His album collaborations reflected the depth of Black musical expression with rising figures in Zlatan and M.anifest via West Africa, seminal stalwarts in Angelique Kidjo and Damian Marley and perhaps the newest direction of them all, the presence of African-American artists in YG, Future and Jeremih. In an interview with *The Atlantic* Burna Boy described the presence of African American musicians on the album as, 'bringing my brothers home.' Musically the album reflects its features in that it is a fusion of multiple Black genres with Africanness being at the core. In terms of its content Burna Boy displays versatility. The album on the one hand was reflective and educational touching on topics such as corruption within Nigeria, the economic legacy of his country, the struggles of living back home and Black spirituality. The album was also celebratory and joyous exploring Black joy, love and perseverance. The album would lead to Burna Boy's first appearance on America's hit show *The Jimmy Kimmel Show*, another crossover moment for the artist who performed his song 'Anybody' to an eager and intrigued American audience. The album was critically acclaimed and largely seen as a crossover success. Burna Boy would gain a grammy nomination for the album, which would be the fourth Grammy nomination for a Nigerian artist in the history of the Grammys. In what seemed to be the perfect way to end the album, the voice of Burna Boy's manager, more affectionately known as his mother, plays. The last song on the album *Spiritual* ends with a sound clip of Mama Burna from her 2019 acceptance speech for Burna Boy's Best International Act award at the BET Awards. In the soundclip, she reminds listeners that Black people were African before they were anything else.

Perhaps just as impactful as his own music is the role Burna Boy plays as a influential feature artist. Some of his memorable features include UK rapper Dave's single 'Location', which peaked at No. 6 on the UK singles charts, UK rapper Stormzy's single 'Own It', which peaked at No. 1 on the UK singles chart and Afro-swing artist J Hus's single 'Play Play', which charted at No. 1 on the UK singles charts.

In April 2020, during the first lockdown in the UK, I took

to one of the video call platforms to speak to one half of one of the most influential groups in African music. Wale Davies better known as 'Tec' of the band Show Dem Camp hails from a creative family that had a connection to music in Nigeria. Show Dem Camp are a rap duo based in Nigeria, which includes Ghost (aka Olumide Ayeni), and were formed in the late 2000s. Like Burna Boy, Wale Davies also comes from a family with deep links to Nigerian music. 'My dad used to manage an artist called King Sunny Ade who's quite a big artist in Nigeria. Earlier on in his life he used to be the Motown Records rep for West Africa, so he would get the vinyls and authorise licensing.' He adds, 'We have a picture of Stevie Wonder in our house in Nigeria... when he came for FESTAC '77, I think Motown had connected him with the rep in Nigeria, which was my Dad so he was the one who would take him around to the Shrine [and] to different places'.

It's this subconscious influence that has seen Wale Davies navigate the juxtaposition of global Blackness through the confident African-American lens and spending his own form-ative years in Lagos, London and Dublin. Wale Davies lived in Dublin during his mid-teens. Dublin would be a place where Davies first encountered life as a minority and subsequently made a commitment to reaffirm his culture going forward. He recalls, 'I [was] the anomaly in the situation. So we would cling on even though there were four of us [Black kids] in the school and we would cling on to Black culture, so we would be blaring hip hop at them and teach them about hip hop.' Davies adds, 'in Dublin so many people would pronounce my name like Wally, so I would change my name to Sean as it was easier ... growing up it almost felt like everything African was local in a way and I didn't really want to identify with it.'

Wale Davies, like many Black music fans of that time, admits to rapping in an American or British accent until a fellow Nigerian friend at university introduced him to a DVD which included rising Nigerian artists in 2Face and Sound Sultan in the early 2000s. The former in particular had a profound influence on Wale, noting his deep commentary on society in Nigeria and politics, and giving him an introduction to a new scene with fresh sounds emerging.

After a brief hiatus from music in his mid-20s, Davies took to working in the finance industry. He would eventually take a three month sabbatical and return to Nigeria to work on a national tour in 2008 with Olumide Ayeni, aka Ghost, who is the other half of Show Dem Camp. The tour spanned over six Nigerian states complete with a new wave of established and upcoming musicians including the aforementioned 2Face, Nneka, P-Square, D'Banj and more. The multi-city tour was the first of its kind in 20 years and largely based around university campuses.

Show Dem Camp was a name as much as it was a mantra that embodied the sentiment of proving naysayers wrong. For Davies and Ayeni in particular, this meant perseverance against parental dissaproval about them pursuing a musical career and pushing back against the music industry who dismissed them as being 'rich kids'. Davies explains, 'We kind of had to adopt this siege mentality and show everybody and do our thing. For us it's like how do we equally support the next person coming up or how do we help shine a light on this other person. That's really been the ethos of everything we've been doing.'

Their early underground success came from their *Clone Wars* mixtape series, first released in 2010. Show Dem Camp were an example of a group unapologetically embracing the sonics of their travels with Southern rap, dubstep and indie rockstar aesthetics. The refreshing lyricism of the group came at a time where other Black men were displaying vulnerability in their music, this includes artists like Kid Cudi, Frank Ocean, Drake and the list goes on. Their musical expression in this sense was an early iteration of the West African alté scene that would emerge years later, where sensitivity, uniqueness and honesty would be an accepted.

Show Dem Camp's debut album *The Dreamer Project* released in 2011. It was a departure that resonated with a younger demographic across Nigeria and beyond. The album was a reflection on multiple journeys of dreamers and those wanting to escape their current circumstances pursuing seemingly unattainable goals. However, it was the 2013 release of their single 'Feel Alright', with its highlife guitar riffs and spaced out hip hop drums, that saw Show Dem Camp land on a gentle and melodic sound that was danceable whilst being a fresh tribute to the sounds of the past. The track featured fellow Nigerian artists Boj and Poe with the production handled by the versatile Juls.

The story of how Show Dem Camp got their hands on a Juls produced beat was one of chance. Ghanaian artist Efya gave the duo a CD of Juls produced instrumentals. A friend of Davies would one day be using his laptop when he played the instrumentals. Impressed by the music, Davies' friend notified him—the rest was history. Davies recalls the moment his friend heard the instrumentals: 'He said bro I just heard something on your laptop and the thing was on shuffle and I heard this beat. I don't know what it is, but you guys have to rap on this beat and I was like okay cool. When I got back home, I asked him what the beat is and he said it's called Track 2... I heard it and I was like wow I never heard this and then I started coming up with ideas for it.' This breakthrough sound would inform the vibe for subsequent projects such as both volumes of *Palm Wine Music* released in 2017 and 2018 alongside the *Palm Wine Express* released in 2019. Both volumes would focus on Nigerian identity. Davies adds, 'we spoke about *Palm Wine* and for me *Palm Wine* is not just about music. It's almost like reverse engineering. Everything we have in Nigeria is brought into our space, like the clothes we wear. Jeans. Vans. Nike. Moët. Hennessy.' He further explains, 'these are the things we champion in Nigerian music in general so for me in the wider context and the way the world is going… [it] is a sense of ownership and promoting and projecting our culture.'

The *Palm Wine* series would also personify the group's open door policy for collaboration with a number of artists from the alternative scene in West Africa including Tems, Odunsi (The Engine), Worlasi, Ajebutter, Amaarae and Lady Donli. The growth of this audio experience would later culminate in the duo launching their inaugural Palm Wine Festival in Lagos in 2017. Davies notes an influential Black British group as an inspiration for the *Palm Wine* vision, 'I've seen in the garage times how So Solid would move and you would have Oxide and Neutrino doing the same show. Then they would have Ms Dynamite and trying to build on that because the culture is not big enough for us to all try and stand alone.'

Show Dem Camp represented Nigeria and West Africa in new ways but were always informed by the traditions of their heritage.

With hospitable mentors like Show Dem Camp new and emerging Afrobeats and African artists will continue to embody this stronghold of legacy in the decades to come.

10
DIASPORIC SOUNDS, AFRO-SUFFIXES AND EVERYTHING IN BETWEEN

Names are a powerful thing, they can serve as a prequel to deep dialogue and coincidently be an ice breaker to defrost unknown territory of introducing yourself to new people. Early grime heads remember Wiley's 'Wot Do U Call It?', released in 2004, which samples his own classic instrumental 'Eskimo'. It attempted to explain the sum of a new genre still taking baby steps via the mixture of influences which itself emerged through UK garage, 2-step and jungle. These genres in their infancy were largely dominated by the sons, daughters and grandchildren of the Windrush generation. Ironically, Wiley never mentions grime once in the lyrics and harks back to reclaiming his own sound by the routine proclamation of 'Eski' at the start of his songs. It's a prevalent feature across his weighty discography built over the last two decades and reclaiming a movement that was undergoing an early identity crisis whilst simultaneously being on the cusp of crossing over to the mainstream.

Defining a movement especially around music of Black origin always straddles the danger of representing Blackness as a monolith, reconstituting its rawness for the purpose of palatability for middle class audiences. Nearly two decades later, Afrobeats and the many subgenres are now encountering the same debate that grime did. What do we indeed call it? These conversations are an organic consequence of being an influential strand of popular culture among young people.

This is a common challenge for cultural explosions in Britain where the relationship between Blackness via Africa and/the Caribbean is still seen or felt through the spectre of a colonial past. The reality of course is that music overtly mirrors migration and the current artists that sit under the Afro-swing umbrella are the sum of that experience in adulthood articulating their truths which parents of an older generation previously considered taboo topics.

The question Wiley posits may be deemed as tongue in cheek on the surface yet in the same instance it's a reactionary retort against the misrepresentation which applies to the moniker of Afrobeats and the subsequent suffixes of Afro-bashment, Afro-swing, Afro-pop, Afrobbean and even Afro-trap.

There has been ample pushback from those definitively deemed 'Afrobeats' artists against the name. The conversation has inevitably trickled down into the suffixed genres that have come after it also.

The first part of the word Afro, is overwhelmingly agreed on. Afro by definition is connected to or with Africa which is at the core of what Afrobeats and the other suffixes are about. Part of the issue arises from the insinuation that a name provides a static representation of something that is far more fluid and constantly evolving. The music we are discussing does after all provide an immediate soundtrack and resolute commentary on Black life in Britain, Africa and abroad where the suffixes are in a state of flux.

When focusing the lens on the UK, within London in particular we have seen how the Afrobeats scene has grown and continues to develop. It is due to its development that new names have entered denoting newer subgenres of Afro-pop, Afro-bashment and Afro-rap. The hyphenated terms at a minimum do a decent job in capturing something that is difficult to encapsulate for listeners whilst giving music labels the language they need to categorise and package Black sounds for listeners. From a societal point of the view, the prefix of the word 'Afro' alongside the hyphenated suffixes serves as a bridge to the subgenres they borrow from.

The most common subgenre in terms of its usage in the UK at the time of writing this book is Afro-swing, with artists J Hus, Kojo Funds and Yxng Bane, all considered pioneers of the genre. The term Afro-swing emanated from East London artist Kojo Funds, himself of Dominican and Ghanaian heritage, who used it to define his sound. The influence of Afrobeats and dancehall in his music alongside the balance of African-American sounds is a notable departure deeply embedded within the soundtrack of African homes and hall parties growing up. Kojo Funds is on record stating, 'You get a new jack swing vibe and R&B vibe mixed in as well. That's the "swing" part of it.'

Here I will delve into a few influential artists that reflect the early embers of the Afro-swing sound and its development in the present day.

SNEAKBO

At the start of the last decade in 2010, I was 21 years old and in my last year of university. It was a time when side pouches were in vogue and music sounded best only if played on the loudspeaker of your mobile phone, at the back of the bus. This was the same year Gordon Brown's Labour party exited Downing Street with the Conservatives and Liberal Democrats forming a coalition government, it would also be the year that the infamous student-led protests occurred in Central London. A rebellious response to rising university tuition fees that would ensue, with portable speakers on rolling trolleys pumping out UK rap music. 2010, was an eventful year, politically, economically and culturally.

In that same year, on the Angell Town Estate in Brixton, a rapper named Sneakbo started to make waves. Known for early hits 'Wave Like Us' and 'Touch Ah Button', Sneakbo was born Agassi Babatunde Odusina and would become a prominent force within the trajectory of UK, though this wasn't something that was abundantly clear at first.

At first glance, the video to Sneakbo's song 'Wave Like Us' serves as an archetypal UK rap visual of its time. Mandem are wearing sunglasses at night, layered up in hoodies and thick jackets doing their best impressions of the Michelin Man on the block. Fellow rapper Political Peak, begins the song stating his alliterative name with gleaming bravado. The beat produced by South London producer Dego Brown, uses a sample taken from US hip hop group Army of the Pharaoh's song 'Seven', speeding it up and altering the drums.

The song itself laid passage to the iconic Sneakbo line 'Jetski wanna dagga dagga dat', a musical phrase that remains etched in UK road rap history. The term 'Jetski Wave' became synonymous with Sneakbo and even made its way all across the Atlantic to a then rising star in rap music, Aubrey 'Drake' Graham who first enrolled on his London Road Culture conversion course by famously tweeting, 'on a jet ski wave… word to Sneaky,' in 2011.

'Wave Like Us' was an early example of UK rappers spraying the beat with the cadence of a Jamaican MC with Sneakbo confidently announcing bars like, 'she she wan do me' and 'she wan do the boogie.' The contents of 'Wave Like Us', are in some ways typical of an archetypal rap song in that it touches on the subjects of being desired by women, generating money and eliminating enemies.

TOUCH AH BUTTON

'Honestly I don't think the Afroswing [sic] we listen to today would exist without these man. Real UK pioneers bmt,' says a YouTube user named Payman commenting underneath the song 'Touch Ah Button'. This song would go on to solidify Sneakbo's early home-grown status within the UK music scene. In June 2010, the BB (Blackberry) anthem 'Touch Ah Button' from the *I'm Buzzin'* mixtape was released and the Black UK music scene would never be the same again. The song, a remix of dancehall O.G. Vybz Kartel's 'Touch Ah Button', heard Sneakbo introduce the song in one of the most memorable ways ever, 'Sneakbo let me show you the wave,' who goes on to rapping his classic refrain 'Jetski gotta dagga dagga dat.' The proud Brixton native of Nigerian heritage found the Vybz Kartel beat on YouTube before creating the track with fellow rappers JJ and Political Peak.

The song instantly clicked and became a street classic and is often cited as one of the integral records of the UK road rap scene. The song was a cultural moment and its impact a decade later has unmistakably influenced the aforementioned Afro-swing sound which exists today. Though he didn't make much money from the song itself, Sneakbo attests that it remains his 'biggest song' in a 2018 Tim Westwood interview, maintaining that whenever he performs it, crowds recite the whole verse. If you are a millennial of the middle range who at some point was raving in the early Noughties, you can attest to the wildfire reaction that Touch Ah Button still receives when a DJ juggles the crossfader to elicit an acapella response from partygoers.

Sneakbo's 'Touch Ah Button' perfectly personified the organic influence of Black migration from Africa and the Caribbean on multicultural London. Giving a nod to its wider impact on British culture following the lineage of Smiley Culture, Roots Manuva, Dizzee and Kano. Brixton historically was referred to as the 'Little Jamaica of London', due to its huge Jamacian population and in turn, Jamaican-owned clothing boutiques, record shops and restaurants, making a new home away from home. As has been mentioned throughout the book, London is a city that boasts a rich Black diasporic culture which has served as a meeting point where Africans and Caribbeans have sought a radical self-actualisation. It is therefore not at all surprising that Sneakbo's introduction of melodic street music fused with African and Caribbean influences was instantly taken to by listeners from the Big Smoke and other cities across the UK, including Birmingham, Manchester and Leeds, which all share a similar migration pattern.

As well as cementing Sneakbo as a pioneering figure in the UK rap scene, 'Touch Ah Button' was the prequel to a musical matrimony of sounds that were not yet swimming in the 'mainstream'.

The music video, at the time of writing this book, sits on 1.8 million views, which is lower than its true viewership, a common downside of UK rappers having their videos taken down by police on YouTube.

The marriage between Sneakbo and diasporic Black sounds would continue throughout his music. A couple of years after 'Touch Ah Button', Sneakbo released a remix to the Afrobeats song Oliver Twist by D'Banj. The remix reached D'Banj who admired his take and asked Sneakbo to make an appearance in the official music video. Sneakbo has publicly professed his love for Afrobeats in several interviews, claiming in a 2018 interview with *Trench Magazine,* 'Afrobeats is in me.' He has further built upon his legacy as a pioneer in the present day by featuring on the Team Salut-produced Afrowave banger 'Stay Winning' by Afro B and Team Salut as well as his own single 'Gang', collaborating with the new wave of Ghanaian artists Kwesi Arthur and Darkovibes on an Afro-trap production courtesy of Kuvie.

TIMBO

As with all cultural phenomenons, it is rarely ever the case that one particular person is solely responsible for its existence. When it comes to examining the impact of pioneering artists of the Afro-suffixed sound, it is essential to look at another musician who also hails from South London. This artist goes by the name of Timbo from the STP movement, an acronym that stood for Stack That Paper crew before it took on a new meaning in the updated acronym Struggle to Proceed. Timbo STP also known as Mr Aleyeleye was born and bred in SE1 and started his music career at university.

Timbo's verse on the 'Qwik Freestyl' is often heralded as an underground freestyle classic that was significant in the trajectory of the Afro-swing genre. The video to the freestyle was filmed in Waterloo SE1 and features the artist wearing a North Face cap alongside his fellow STP members Cass, Mitch and other mandem. Timbo's verse was just over a minute long yet it was enough time to lay the beat with his infectious West African twang and renowned 'ay-leh-leh-lay' ad-lib, which he explained in a 2015 interview with Uncle Rafool meant 'faaji', which is the Yoruba term for 'enjoyment'. Timbo's artistry continued the evolution of Afrobeats mixing with UK music, sprinkling his Afro influence via his signature ad-libs and melodic hooks on early tracks such as 'Ringtone'. The catchy and melodic nature of Timbo's flow exported African style over Caribbean beats whilst harnessing UK street culture— once again, providing a musical marriage that was apt for the UK.

Timbo has been open about Nigeria being a major influence on his music, praising artists like Fela Kuti, Wizkid and DBanj. The combination of his delivery, African swagger and London street style is a trope that still permeates Afro-swing today.

At the time of Timbo's emergence in the music scene the labels and definitions that exist today had not yet come into fruition. In a 2016 interview with BnG, Timbo explained that his sound was not simple to label, admitting that grime artists saw him as an Afrobeats artist and Afrobeats artists saw him as a grime artist. An assertion that perfectly captures the amalgamated nature of the Afro-suffixed sound in its early days and also one that shows Timbo was ahead of his time.

NAIRA MARLEY

Another individual who has since managed to maintain his clutch on cultural and musical relevance is Lagos born Afeez Fashola, more commonly known as Naira Marley. Marley moved to Peckham, South London at the age of 11—and his debut hit 'Marry Juana', released in 2015, would become a cult riddim loaded with clever double-entendres and a proud African intonation.

It turns out that the creation of the song was an unplanned occurrence. It was the result of a studio session Naira Marley had organised not for himself but for his friends who he felt were the talented ones. In that session, a friend encouraged him to record the spaces in a song, which gave Naira the lightbulb moment to pursue music seriously. He then recorded his own song, 'Marry Juana' with Max Twigz. Naira Marley's melodic approach fused with his Nigerian flow and accent resulted in the song becoming an instant success.

Marley's unapologetic Nigerian accent riding over a dance-hall inspired beat equipped with the South London street style is once again a nod to the the union of African identity and Caribbean identity that now exists in Black Britain. Naira Marley's name itself is also an emblem of the growing fusion of African and Caribbean culture within Britain. Naira being the currency of Nigeria and Marley being the surname of the famous Jamaican artist Bob Marley. Considering all of the above, it should be of no surprise therefore that Naira Marley's 'Marry Juana' is considered one of the early examples of the Afro-suffixed subgenre—Afro-bashment.

The progress of information technology in the beginning of the Noughties, where Blackberry (BBM) messaging was a precursor to WhatsApp, allowing people to share music links with peers and beyond, would lead to folks inadvertently creating their own social network. This would occur alongside the early stages of this musical subculture. In August 2011, an Ofcom study found that the Blackberry was the smartphone of choice for the majority of British teenagers. In the aftermath of the London riots in the same year, the Blackberry was seen as a facilitator of social unrest due to its private and secure network allowing untraceable BBM messages to be spread across the capital without interception from authorities. This was a key function of the Blackberry owing to its roots as a device for the corporate world. Yet working class youth would reimagine this technology shifting its use from a business communication gadget to a music sharing device linking artists and fans in their own virtual fan clubs. This would cut out the middleman, where grassroots artists would access instant feedback to new tracks. This in turn allowed for a sense of exclusivity for a burgeoning underground base to grow without major label interference.

Fast-forward to the middle of the decade, where advanced smartphones and the widespread availability of 4G mobile data enables tracks to be shared more quickly via various methods, including streaming platforms with dedicated play-lists, including the Afro-bashment playlist on Spotify and the Afro-swing playlist on Apple Music.

J HUS

The bonafide king of what many call Afro-swing, and right-fully so, is Momodou Jallow, better known as J Hus. 2015 would herald the release of his first mixtape *15th Day*. The mixtape was full of strong records, but one in particular would take the UK by storm. The record in question was titled, 'Dem Boy Paigon'. Sonically it was an African and Caribbean con-vergence filled with guiding interpolations from Beenie Man's classic 'Who I Am?' and I-Wayne's 'Can't Satisfy Her' respec-tively. The self proclaimed 'Uglyboy' of Gambian heritage spits in Pidgin, 'are you mad, you dey craze,' with the hook professing his inability to trust people around him. The rise and success of J Hus has pushed him to the forefront of the UK industry, now becoming a national treasure.

Like those who came before him, J Hus has developed and pushed forth the Afro-fusion sound and much like Timbo, Naira Marley and even Sneakbo, Hus uses African intona-tions, accents, and language, fusing them with London street culture. Across his artistry, Hus can be found spitting and singing in Patois, Pidgin, and English. In December 2019, J Hus tweeted, 'if I'm being honest, Sneakbo & Naira Marley set the pace. Then I came after,' a nod to the pioneers that came before him.

Part of Hus's prophetic genius comes from his ability to communicate words, ideas and phrases that in turn become entrenched in culture. He has an almost hypnotic superpower, whether it be his 'husla bay-beh' adlib, which according to tweets from the artist he has since retired or his infamous claim 'I like my fanta with no h'ice', not to forget his many aliases including 'Bouff Daddy, Juju J, Fisherman, Lead Militerian of the Jamba Boys'.

It would be easy to write a book on the brilliance and catchiness of J Hus lyrics, (who knows maybe one day there will be *A Quick Ting On: J Hus Lyrics*), but I digress. In the same way Sneakbo proudly states Afrobeats is in him and Timbo and Naira hold their Nigerian heritage close, J Hus's unique artistry can be credited to his proud Gambian heritage, African pride and diasporic upbringing in the UK.

J Hus was born and raised in London, his mother landed in London from Gambia as a young 25 year old and regularly took a young J Hus to African hall parties, an experience that Hus recites in interviews often. This musical influence existed against the backdrop of iconic Black artists like Michael Jackson and Bob Marley. Hus, an East Londoner, was also taking in the regional sonics of grime and UK rap, and the final element of his musical arsenal was when Hus was introduced to 50 Cent's *Get Rich or Die Trying* album, one of the most renowned Gangsta rap albums of all time.

If there was a magical music machine that could mix up African music with the likes of Michael Jackson, 50 Cent, UK grime and rap, J Hus's artistry could well be the result.

Today, J Hus is a figure larger than life, which is even more interesting considering his sporadic use of social media, very rarely posting online. Hus is a creative catalyst within the UK and one who shows no signs of slowing down. In the history books (including this one) Hus will be remembered as a key artist in the subgenre of Afro-swing and more generally UK music. At the time of writing this book, J Hus has only released two albums, *Common Sense* released in 2017 and *Big Conspiracy* released in 2020 yet his dominance is unwavering. Hus's career still being in its infancy is impressive when considering the weight of his impact in a relatively short space of time.

Common Sense was J Hus's debut album released in May 2017. The album featured heavy production from Jae5, alongside verses from other British and African heavyweights in MoStack and Burna Boy. The abum would receive excellent reviews and chart at number six on the UK Albums Charts. The album single, 'Did You See', would chart an impressive at number nine on the UK Singles Chart. An excellent feat for the artist's first album.

Big Conspiracy would be Hus's second studio album released in January 2020. The album charted at number one on the UK Charts and two singles from the album 'No Denying' and 'Must Be' would make it onto the top 40 of the UK Singles Chart. *Big Conspiracy* received critical acclaim from reviewers and in 2021 the album received a Brit nomination for British Album of the Year.

J Hus's third album is one of the most heavily awaited albums in the UK and as I write this book, tweets, articles and videos are regularly released speculating on when the Gambian superstar will drop his latest work.

J Hus has a cult like fan base in the UK and abroad. One of his most famous fans is none other than rapper Drake. The Canadian megastar, would give J Hus an excellent welcome on stage at the 02 arena in April 2019 when Hus was released from prison. This would be a moment that set Black Twitter ablaze and is seen as a watershed moment in the internationality of Black British music.

In 2020 J Hus entered the fashion world, releasing his clothing line 'The Ugliest'. The clothing line sold out shortly after its release. So, what does the future hold for J Hus? It is hard to predict, but no doubt a long career that will continue to push musical and cultural boundaries.

The release of the first official UK Afrobeats compilation *Moves: The Sound of UK Afrobeats Volume 1* in May 2017 showcased a range of Black sounds including highlife riffs and dancehall cadences via Yoruba & Twi colloquialisms. The compilation was released by MOVES Recordings, an independent label based in London, started in late 2016 by Kofi Kyei, Sasha and Ian McQuaid. It was the prequel to a fusion heralding the evolution of a sound that was then maturing. The accompanying copy noticeably included 'Africa, The Caribbean And The Ends' as geographical reference points and was curated by Ross-Emmanuel Bayeto better known as Afro B.

Previously a DJ on the university rave circuit playing a number of Anglophone and Francophone African styles, Afro B would soon become an artist releasing early UK Afrobeats bangers in 'Baba God', 'Personal Lover' and 'Juice & Power'.

The biggest hit for the artist of Ivorian heritage would be 'Joanna (Drogba)' produced by regular production collaborators Team Salut. The opening onomatopoeic ad-libs are whispery enzymes that accelerate both eardrums and heart rate. A mellow meander led by icy and glacial chords lulls you until the chorus revs with a drum kick full of vim.

Its early popularity originating from a Homebros dance class and the subsequent creation of the #DrogbaChallenge took the banger outside the confines of a club setting to NBA arenas, football dressing rooms and beyond. The singalong clarity of the hook and the blank canvas of adding your own choreography to the song created an expansive outreach for the record. Peaking at No. 23 on the US *Billboard* R&B/hip hop Airplay Chart, 'Joanna''s global impact has seen a range of likely and unlikely remix versions from the NBA legend Shaquille O' Neal, to a collaboration with Puerto Rican star Ozuna for a global Latin version.

Other notable Afro-fusion riddims to emerge from the second half of the Noughties include Not3s' 'Addison Lee', B Young's, 'Jumanji', 'Barking' by Ramz, Belly Squad's 'Banana Remix', Hardy Caprio's 'Best Life', Kojo Funds 'Dun Talkin' with Abra Cadabra, Yxng Bane's 'Fine Wine' feat. Kojo Funds, Krept & Konan's 'G Love' feat. Wizkid, NSG's 'Options', 'OT Bop' and Yo Darlin' feat. Geko and Don-E & Nado's 'You Alrite Yh'. This blended discography marks the growing influence of African music in the UK and highlights the ways in which Black British artists acknowledge contemporary African sonics adding to it, their own twist.

Before the Afrobeats boom, school playgrounds for Black youth were arenas for spitting grime freestyles (rapping in cypher style) against 140 BPM instrumentals (usually blaring from our Sony Ericsson Walkmans). The shift in the creative expression amongst the same demographic; this time, to Afrobeats would be an interesting development. Instead of spraying bars in the playgrounds, Black youth were now partaking in a number of Afrobeats skanks and singing Afrobeats songs.

The warm diasporic sound of the Afro-suffixed subgenres has allowed for a wider range of topics to be explored in the music. Unlike the content limitation of other Black youth led genres such as grime or drill, subgenres like Afro-swing have allowed the archetypal subject of love to be centred, resulting in women taking ownership and adding their own 'sauce'.

Examples of this include Not3s and Mabel's hit 'My Lover' , Mabel and Kojo Funds's single 'Finders Keepers' and Yxng Bane and Kojo Funds single 'Fine Wine'. The centering of love and romance in Afro sounding music can similarly be found in the British-Ghanaian artist Raye's song 'Confidence', produced by Nana Rogues featuring Maleek Berry and Ms Banks's single 'Snack' featuring Kida Kudz produced by Guiltybeatz.

A special mention to Afroswing artist Darkoo, someone who defies gender boundaries and blessed us with the Year of Return anthem in 'Gangsta', a song that peaked at number 22 on the UK Singles Chart, and charted at number one, on the UK Afrobeats Chart in 2020. Another riddim that not only offers an exploration of love but also epitomises that linkup between Africa and the Caribbean is 'LoveStruck' from West London group WSTRN featuring Tiwa Savage and Mr Eazi. Haile and Mr Eazi fuse a silky hook marinated in Patois and Pidgin and Tiwa shells down a dreamy verse with Louie's sparring flow. Outside of London, Young T and Bugsey and PA Salieu from the East Midlands further exemplify that scenes outside the capital can develop just as organically. The former duo from Nottingham came to prominence filming on the block with the memorable 'Gangland' and now sit on the aforementioned Black Butter Records releasing popular saccharine hits in 'Ay Caramba', 'Strike A Pose' and the lockdown hit 'Don't Rush' featuring rapper Headie One.

 PA Salieu,was raised in Coventry and is of Gambian heritage. His infectious flow often incorporates English alongside Pidgin on songs like 'Frontline'. PA Salieu like his fellow Gambian artist J Hus credits his Gambian identity as a large part of his self actualisation.

A decade on from those early hood videos where the confidence of Sneakbo to lead the wave would soon cause others to ride and follow their own paths, has now led us here. The evolution of Black British music has been a brilliant tale so far. Writer Ciaran Thapar states, 'if someone wants something more gritty and hyper-modern, they turn to drill. If someone wants to vibe and dance, they turn to Afro-bashment.' It's a reflective statement that takes in the level of choice now at our disposal in this streaming era.

The journey of Black British music coming into contemporary African music has allowed for the healthy expansion of the Black experience through relatable artists who steer away from monolithic descriptions of culture. It is what makes the UK a particuarly exciting location for the growth of future Black sounds

However we feel about the Afro suffixed labels, one thing is for certain, the modern iteration of the Afro sound has cemented modern Africanness into the musical ether. This was no easy journey and many have been responsible for getting it this far. Just as those before them, the next generation of African artists (regardless of birthplace) will continue pushing their creativity to the forefront giving music lovers newer expressions of what it means to be African in the modern age.

11

HOMECOMING AND THE FUTURE

In the UK, when one becomes an adult it is commonplace to go on a trip with friends during the Summer break. This is usually an all-inclusive package deal or improvised no frills departure to the destinations of Ayia Napa, Malia, Zante or other similar European locations.

What is usually on offer? The roasting hot climate, alcohol, relatively cheap food, sex and the influx of underground artists from the UK garage, grime and funky scene. The trip is promised to be a hedonistic haven without the gaze of your snooping parents and other snitching family members. Yet, in the last five years there has been a gradual shift in UK born West African youth, who do not seem to be interested in booking a cheeky flight to Ayia Napa, and no, it isn't because the UK has left the EU. It is in fact because they have turned their direction toward different cities like Accra and Lagos in Africa.

For me, this 'going back home' trip happened in December 2014. Though I was initially reluctant to switch up my usual Christmas routine, the trip felt necessary. It seems silly to say something was in the air but at the time this is how it felt. Home was calling and so I went! I wasn't the only one, the post-azonto era seemed to bring with it a sense of longing in many youngsters of West African origin. African identity was mainstream and the final phase would be to go back home.

We saw the global success of Marvel's *Black Panther* and the crossover of African artists on the aforementioned superhero soundtrack including South African rapper Sjava and 'gqom queen' Babes Wodumo. After this would come the Beyoncé co-signed *Lion King* soundtrack that included Burna Boy and Ghanaian artist Shatta Wale. The world, outside of Africans, it seemed, was calling for Africa.

The Year of Return was proposed by Ghanaian President Nana Akuffo-Addo in 2018 for the following year. It was initially set up to commemorate 400 years of the arrival of the first enslaved Africans in Jamestown, Virginia in 1619. The initiative was created to, 'celebrate the cumulative resilience of all the victims of the Transatlantic Slave'. Therefore, this open call welcomed all people of African origin to return to Ghana. The Year of Return attracted some of the world's biggest Black names including model Naomi Cambell, rapper Cardi B, actor Idris Elba and many more. There was even a rumour that Beyoncé would be in attendance, leading to hotels being booked up 6 months in advance. Actors and musicians alike held an array of events, including Fuse ODG's T.I.N.A. festival. The Year of Return was widely seen as a success, with reports that it had injected roughly £1.5bn into the Ghanaian economy.

Then there was AfroNation. After a successful European edition in summer of 2019 at the Algarve, Portugal, where AfroNation hosted over 20,000 fans from across the African diaspora, they decided to bring the festival to Ghana. This would be the first time the music festival was on African soil. AfroNation, which now claims to be the biggest Afrobeats festival in the world, originated from the ACS university rave scene in the UK .

The co-founder of AfroNation was born Adesegun Adeosun Jr, better known as SMADE. He moved to the UK at

19 and became known for hosting the best parties on campus as a student from 2005 to 2009 at The University of The Arts in London.

In the aftermath of the 2019 Year of Return in Ghana, I speak to the Nigerian entrepreneur on a damp January afternoon over the phone in 2020. A reflective query into SMADE's early childhood in Nigeria provides insight into his approach in later decades, 'my dad is the biggest inspiration. [He] used to listen to Fela and Ebenezer Obey… He would get us to compete with one another… dance and all that stuff so it was quite entertaining.' He adds, 'he used to make all his kids pick a profession and I was the accountant of the household. There was a lot of discipline in the household that still follows me everywhere.'

Once SMADE's secondary school education was complete in Nigeria, he would move to London in 2004 and study Marketing, ending up with a Masters from the Greenwich School of Management in 2015. During this time SMADE would be balancing jobs in care work and retail. His hard working mentality would soon prove effective in his future entertainment exploits. SMADE goes on to state, 'in terms of music, I worked in the HMV factory, which [helped] educate me, and care work would help me care more about people no matter the age or culture.' This personability would also be the trait that led to him hosting house parties as an undergraduate, 'I was passionate about bringing people together and seeing smiles on people's faces.' His own infamous birthday party in university would inadvertently lead to SMADE becoming a promoter in his own right.' I had a very massive birthday party in my house and the police came to me and said, "why don't you take this to a club?" I went to a venue… after I delivered a very good event, the club owners called me back and asked if I was a promoter.' This was during his first year at university and saw the novice enthusiast soon diversify his portfolio into comedy shows, club tours and concerts. The latter sphere would see him work for early Afrobeats promoter CokoBar, assisting them to eventually sell out a D'Banj show in 2009 at the indigo O2 in London.

This initial success would lead to a fruitful partnership in not only promoting himself but establishing relationships for Cokobar with seminal venues such as the Hammersmith Apollo in West London. This would lead to SMADE providing a platform through headline shows for established Afro-pop artists P-Square and hosting a young Wizkid at the Afrobeats Festival in 2011 in London.

SMADE would soon stop working with Cokobar to create his own independent company SMADE Entertainment, which led to him organising a Davido concert in September 2013 at the indigo O2. After nearly a decade-long relationship supporting upcoming artists, the next creative ambition for SMADE was to host a festival. After a meeting with Obi Asika, the CEO of Echo Talent Agency, SMADE would enter a business relationship with the CEO. The two men would become business partners and lay the foundations for what would later become the AfroNation festival. Reflecting on their early plans for the festival, SMADE explains how it began, 'we started making plans and built a big team together who were the best at everything.'

The first AfroNation festival would take place in Portugal in 2019 and it was generally seen as a success. Once the Year of Return in Ghana was announced, SMADE couldn't pass up the opportunity to return to the African continent. SMADE expands on this further, 'Portugal was you going on holiday to see your favourite superstars on stage with your friends. Ghana was more cultural. More family. Finding your roots and understanding the importance of your culture.'

AfroNation in Ghana was complete with a stellar lineup including the 'African Giant' Burna Boy who hypnotised the crowd on sandy terrain. There was a fireworks display during Shatta Wale's performance, a glowing appearance on stage by Nigerian artist Teni and much more.

The success would lead to AfroNation signing an official memorandum a few weeks after the festival's conclusion in early January 2020 to host their festival in Ghana for the next five years as part of its Beyond The Return initiative.

Another important figure who places context at the heart of projecting contemporary music and creativity on the African continent is Mike Calandra Achode. The Benin born, Rome raised and now London based graphic designer and lecturer is the founder of Crudo Volta, a visual collective documenting the development of contemporary musical scenes of the African diaspora. Initially a music producer, he spent formative summers in the banlieues of Paris with extended family members, reconnecting with his Beninese culture.

On the relationship Black people have with music, Achode says 'What I've resolved over the years is that as Black people music is our main literature, language and that's how we speak about everything. If you think about movements like Coupe Decale, for example, brought the street experience of being in France and being in a banlieue, but they wanted to stay African.' He adds, 'they didn't want to become African-Americans and didn't want to rap, but they wanted to rap in their own way. Music was definitely this haven, but the paradox is that music has always been this haven since forever.'

After reconnecting with a mutual friend, Francesco Cucchi (formerly known as producer Nan Kole), in London who was embarking on releasing South African music from Durban via a new record label called Gqom Oh!, Achode turned to documentaries as a forum to explore Black music. He would call it

Taxi. The idea was to go to a specific city in Africa and explore a brewing genre and its history. The official first doc was called *Woza Taxi* (Zulu word meaning come), released in 2016, capturing young producers from the townships in Durban, South Africa.

Subsequent documentaries in the Taxi series have travelled to cities across Africa including Accra in Ghana, Maputo in Mozambique, Lagos in Nigeria and Addis Ababa in Ethiopia. Each documentary projects a new image of Black musical communities away from archaic case studies. Achode's work extinguishes stereotypes reinforced by the vague and limited banner of 'world music' instead shining light on the diverse nature of subcultures within Africa. In 2020, the Crudo Volta collective worked on *Free Borga*, a capsule collaboration across music and fashion with acclaimed Ghanaian streetwear brand Free The Youth. Inspired by the Ghanaian Borga highlife genre where talented musicians from West Africa projected a new identity of what it means to be African in the West. The result was a limited edition t-shirt range with the album artwork of seminal highlife musician Amakye Dede featured and an original compilation album *Heaven's Gate No Bribe* released on independent label Python Syndicate.

A recent branch of the Afrobeats tree which has grown in its own right in the last few years has been the alté movement in Lagos, Nigeria. It is generally accepted that the formation of this scene began in around 2014. A notable moment in the alté movement is in the song 'Paper' by BOJ . On the song he raps, 'the ladies like me because I'm an alté guy.' The term itself is a wider projection of experimental sounds in West Africa. Add in the stylish streetwear swag fused with minimal aesthetics that work to push against any gender norm and attain fluidity at all times. The Nigerian alté movement unapologetically subverts static preconceptions of West African youth culture. The sentiment of the alté movement is that one can be whoever they choose and express themselves freely.

Well known artists from this scene include Wavy The Creator, Odunsi (The Engine), Amaarae, Prettyboy D-O and Lady Donli. Perhaps the most well known alté artist at the moment is Santi. The artist who actually began as a rapper would go on to become the poster boy for the alté movement in Nigeria. His cult alté album *Mandy and The Jungle* was released in May 2019. It was a concept album which explores a fictional extension of the artist. It follows the story of Mandy, a girl who has no idea about the power that lies inside her. The album artwork with its Gothic font filled with 1920s aesthetic is typically dark with Mandy's mouth wide open and shouting. Santi's song 'Rapid Fire', one of the most well known alté songs, sees Santi's patois cadence feature on the hypnotic melody. The song muses on police corruption and hope for a better tomorrow. The album is also home to melodic songs in 'Sparky' and 'Maria'.

In the last five years, the listenership for Afrobeats has grown beyond the usual migrant community. The launch of Spotify's Afro Hub playlist in late 2018 was, in their own words, to be, 'an educational portal, to bring all of these different cultures and communities together from the diaspora.' Their flagship playlist African Heat is one example with the tagline 'Real African vibes, right here. Africa to the world!' The ability to openly track the location of where listeners are consuming music provides an indication as to how far Afrobeats music has come. In an interview at Spotify Headquarters with their former Chief Economist, Will Page, we discussed the streaming popularity of three of the most popular Afrobeats artists on the streaming service, Burna Boy, Davido and Wizkid. It was no surprise that London* led the scoreboard for all three artists, other cities with strong listenership included Paris, Amsterdam and Stockholm. Interestingly, across all different charts there is a notable increase in listenership from North America, in areas such as New York City (Brooklyn in particular), Toronto and Los Angeles.

2020 saw Apple Music launch its first radio show covering African music with DJ Cuppy's show 'Africa Now'. The show is now syndicated to broadcast weekly with Nigeria's Cool FM, one of the most popular stations in Nigeria. 2020 also saw the launch of Def Jam's new division called Def Jam Africa, which was a division based in Lagos and Johannesburg focusing on Afrobeats, hip hop and trap talent from the continent. *Billboard Magazine* had an Afrobeats issue called 'Africa Now' with popular Afrobeats artists Davido, Tiwa Savage and Mr Eazi on the cover feature.

There is a bumpy history of African-American artists collaborating with African artists in an attempt to create the *one* that works. These collaborations, up until recently, lacked consistency and perhaps were ahead of their time. Examples of such collaborations include D'banj's remix to his single 'Mr Endowed' featuring Snoop Dogg released in 2011, Sarkodie's single 'New Guy' featuring Ace Hood released in 2015 and Nigerian group P-Square's single 'Beautiful Onyinye' featuring Rick Ross released in 2012. The latter artists themselves the

---

*   Correct as of April 2019

beneficiaries of signing with Konvict Muzik in Africa alongside 2 Baba (2Face) and a young WizKid. Label Owner Aliaume Damala Badara Akon Thiam, better known as Akon, is of Senegalese descent and has always shown pride in his African heritage. The son of Mor Thiam, an influential drummer who himself settled in the US during the Civil Rights Movement and would often play the djembe drum before their group meetings with other leaders.

In recent times, collaborations between African and American artists have become more frequent. Memorable ones include Wizkid featuring Tems and Justin Bieber on hit song 'Essence', Beyoncé featuring Shatta Wale on the song 'Already', Wizkid featuring Drake on 'Come Closer', Davido featuring Summer Walker on 'D&G', Russ featuring Davido on single 'All I Want', Justin Bieber featuring Burna Boy on 'Loved By You' amongst others.

The African pride of musicians of African heritage runs deep, even within those who do not create music that is considered African. Take Oluowale Victor Akinthemehin for example, better known as the rapper Wale. In an early interview with *the Washington Post*, he assertively told the interviewer 'Allow me to introduce me… my name Wah-lay, don't say wal-ly.' The son of Yoruba migrants, his dad Ayo in the same *Washington Post* feature touches upon where his son's inherent musicality arose from, '[Our family is] from the originators of the talking drums back in Nigeria… It's his inheritance.'

Jidenna, a Nigerian-American artist of Igbo heritage, pivoted further to embracing his West African heritage more overtly. A signee to Janelle Monae's Wondaland Records label, the release of his debut album titled *The Chief,* released in 2017, was a dedication to his late Nigerian father Oliver Mobisson who founded Africa's first computer technology university and would later introduce the first Black African line of PC's known as ASUTECH 800 & 8000. Jidenna would follow his album with his *Boomerang* EP later that year in 2017 featuring Afrobeats artists in stars Maleek Berry and Burna Boy.

The EP would be the prelude to the self exploratory mission Jidenna would reveal on his album *85 to Africa* in 2019. The album is an organic extension of heritage and culture. The title of the album refers to the Interstate 85 highway, which serves major locations in the South-East of the United States and is a popular route to the Charlotte Douglas Airport.

More African-American artists are reorienting their creative catalysts towards Afrobeats. The future is healthy and allows for new iterations of Black expression through art, fashion and film. Already we have seen the early embers of something that is more than just a trend, mirroring movements such as the Harlem Renaissance.

The rise of European-based labels such as Analog Africa, BBE Music and Soundway Records, have studious, crate-digging enthusiasts intrigued enough to pick up reissues of lost classics in the discography of highlife and Afrobeat. This feeds into a new generation of musicians within the 'jazz scene' in London including the Black women led Afrobeat band Kokoroko. In a recent interview I did with bandleader Shelia Maurice Grey she noted the importance of acknowledging the continuity between African music in the past to the present 'jazz is important in terms of its legacy, so is Afrobeat. It's not something which should stay within our parents' generation, especially now with the massive rise of Afrobeats. It's great music, but it's just as important to keep the roots of it alive because politically, socially and historically, it's important music.' She further added, 'it's about keeping that connection and being like, although we haven't lived back home, it's a very important part of our identity and I think that's quite powerful in itself.'

Venues including The Total Refreshment Centre in Stoke Newington, London and nights such as Church of Sound in Clapton, East London (a repurposed holy space turned music venue) have paid homage to African music with nights dedicated to Ebo Taylor and the late Tony Allen. Another notable mention goes to bandleader Wayne Francis and Steamdown, a collective with a mixture of talented African and Caribbean musicians who performed every Wednesday evening in Deptford, South London. The atmosphere is less hedonistic but is comparable to The Shrine in Lagos as a base for therapy through movement in the mid-week.

In February 2021, Spotify announced a groundbreaking expansion into over 80 new global markets with many of those markets located in Sub-Saharan Africa, giving them access to the continent with the world's largest youth population. The previously mentioned flagship playlist *African Heat* is bigger than ever, providing listeners with new African artists and sounds. This African expansion also enables an opportunity to see the growth in the trajectory of other emerging African youth subcultures such as alté music in Nigeria, amapiano music from South Africa and gengetone music from Kenya.

The release of Wizkid's fourth studio album *Made In Lagos* in October 2020 saw the Nigerian artist embrace his roots sonically over 14 tracks. Like Burna Boy's album *African Giant*, *Made in Lagos* features artists from all over the Black Atlantic. Listeners hear Patois and Pidgin over reggae and dancehall inspired tracks in 'Blessed' featuring Damian Marley and 'Smile' with R&B artist H.E.R. With a delayed release dedicated to Nigerians and the #EndSars movement in Nigeria, *Made in Lagos* was a soothing audio antithesis with themes of love, gratitude and grace. Within a week of its release, *Made in Lagos* broke several African streaming records becoming the first African album to debut on the Spotify Global Album chart, and within the top ten at that. The album also surpassed 100 million streams across five platforms nine days after release, a huge milestone for an African artist.

Burnaboy's recent Grammy win for the album *Twice As Tall* in 2021 reflects his growth not only as an African artist but as an International Artist of African heritage. This win would come after the disappointment of *African Giant* not winning the Grammy in 2019. The cover of *Twice As Tall* released in 2020 immortalises Burna Boy as a tall video game character with African monuments including the Pyramids of Egypt in the background. The highway road he treads on is a sign of his ascent to the wider world. The album includes cameos from Coldplay's Chris Martin, rapper Stormzy and executive production from Sean 'Diddy' Combs.

In his award speech he remarked, 'this is a big win for my generation of Africans all over the world, and this should be a lesson to every African out there: no matter where you are, no matter what you plan to do, you can achieve it, no matter where you're from, because you are a king.' His Grammy win, the first for a Nigerian as a solo artist gives a cultural reference point in African musical history that will no doubt inspire other African artists to create projects that appeal to global audiences.

The rise and dominance of this cultural phenomenon called Afrobeats has created a new African economy and world. One where young Africans can become creators, owners, record label executives, festival owners, music producers, directors, artists whilst proudly showcasing their Africanness. To be African and proud on the global stage is a radical sentiment. Africa is being centred on the global stage, not because of struggle, war or famine but because of true Black creativity. The world has come back to the source and the new generation of African artists will continue to create newer expressions and the cultural renaissance shall continue.

Africa to the world. The world to Africa.

REFERENCES

CHAPTER 2

Documentary, *One Day Go Be One Day* by Akinola Davies Jr
Book, *Fela: This Bitch of a Life* by Carlos Moore
Documentary, *Faces of Africa—Fela Kuti: The Father of Afrobeat*, *CGTN Africa*
Article, 'Modern Ghana: Fela Kuti coined Afrobeat in Accra out of hate for James Brown' by Professor John Collins
Article, 'Red Bull Academy, Festac 77' by Uchenna Ikonne

CHAPTER 3

Paper, 'The Nigerian and Ghanaian Gospel Music Explosion' by John Collins
Book, *Highlife Saturday Night*, by Nate Plageman (In 1961, the Arts Council, in an attempt to hinder the dominance of foreign music in Ghana, would encourage dance bands to infuse high-life with traditional dancing and rhythms.)
Paper, 'Popular Performance and Culture in Ghana: The Past 50 Years' by John Collins
Book, *African Pop Roots: The Inside Rhythms of Africa* by John Collins
Book, *The Globalization of Musics in Transit: Music, Migration and Tourism* by Simone Kruger and Ruxandra Trandafoiu
Article, Likembe Blog , 'The Controversial sounds of Burger'
https://likembe.blogspot.com/2018/07/the-controversial-sounds-of-burger.html

CHAPTER 4

Article, Jesse Shipley, 'Part 1. Pan-Africanism and Hiplife'
Article, 'Media in Ghana's Fourth Republic, Broadcasting in Ghana'

CHAPTER 5

Book, *The Original Bob: The story of Bob Johnson, Ghana's Ace Comedian (Makers of Ghanaian theatre)* by Efua Sutherland
Podcast, 'Soul To Soul at 50' by Afropop Worldwide
Book, *African Pop Roots: The Inside Rhythms of Africa* by John Collins
Paper, 'Struggle Music: South African Politics in Song' by Andra Le Roux Kemp
Book, *The Beat that Beat Apartheid: The Role of Music in the Resistance against Apartheid in South Africa* by Anne Schumann
Documentary, *Konkombé: The Nigerian Pop Music Scene* by Jeremy Marre
Paper, 'Yoruba customs and beliefs pertaining to twins' by Fernand Leroy, Taiwo Olaleye-Oruene, Gesina Koeppen-Schomerus, Elizabeth Bryan
Book, *Ibeji custom in Yorubaland* by Timothy Mobolade
Article, Tiwa Savage Interview with Vanguard
https://www.vanguardngr.com/2013/06/my-fiance-wiped-away-my-shame-tiwa-savage/

CHAPTER 6

Podcast, Mo Gilligan with Donae'O
Book, *The African Diaspora Population In Britain* by Martha J. Chinouya and Peter J. Aspinall

CHAPTER 7

Book, *The Music Of Africa* by J.H. Kwabena Nketia
Paper, 'Transnational circulation and digital fatigue in Ghana's azonto dance craze' by Jesse Shipley

CHAPTER 10

Paper, 'The London Clearances, Institute of Race Relations' by Jessica Perera

Book, *Black London: The Imperial Metropolis and Decolonization in the Twentieth Century* by Marc Matera
Book, *The African Diaspora Population In Britain* by Martha J. Chinouya and Peter J. Aspinall
Paper, 'Transnational circulation and digital fatigue in Ghana's azonto dance craze' by Jesse Shipley

CHAPTER 11

Documentary, *Because Of Music: Timbo STP 'I call it a new genre Afro-Hop'*

ACKNOWLEDGMENTS

I would like to thank you, Mum and Dad (Akua and Yaw), Nicole, Kwaku, Kwabena and Kieoni who have always reaffirmed their belief in my dreams and never allowed me to leave my childlike state of curiosity. You've made me proud to embrace my heritage through my creativity.

Shoutout to the visionary Mags for allowing me to be a part of her *A Quick Ting On* series and for publishing my first book!

Lastly, big thank you to the ever-young James Barnor. I'm lucky enough to call you a great friend. May God continue to bless you as much as you've blessed us with your presence.

ABOUT THE AUTHOR

Christian Adofo is a writer, journalist and curator, with a passion for writing about the intersection of heritage and identity in music and culture. His writing has appeared in *The Guardian*, *OkayAfrica* and *Straight No Chaser*, marking him as a key commentator on the seminal figures and burgeoning creative talents within the African diaspora. He has appeared as a guest speaker and host on *BBC Radio*, *Worldwide FM* and *NTS Radio*, discussing Black identity and its impact on culture in the UK and abroad. He has written scripts for BBC series *Black Earth Rising* and the award-winning *Damilola: Our Loved Boy*. In 2017, Christian produced and hosted discussions at Autograph around the 60th anniversary of Ghana's independence, exploring how identity informs the creative practice of young Londoners who share dual heritage. In 2018, he played an Afrobeats inspired DJ set at the Tate Modern as part of their Counterpoint series celebrating the rise of jazz-inspired musicians in London. Christian has also delivered workshops around identity and storytelling with Talawa Theatre Company, and was recently featured in the 2020 Youtube show *A Day In the Life* with Wizkid.